#1

Be
on
Google

52 Fast and Easy
Search Engine Optimization Tools
to Drive Customers to Your Web Site

Jon Smith

New York   Chicago   San Francisco   Lisbon   London
Madrid   Mexico City   Milan   New Delhi   San Juan
Seoul   Singapore   Sydney   Toronto

The McGraw·Hill Companies

Copyright © 2010 by Infinite Ideas Ltd. All rights reserved. Printed in the United States of America. Except as permitted under the United States Copyright Act of 1976, no part of this publication may be reproduced or distributed in any form or by any means, or stored in a data base or retrieval system, without the prior written permission of the publisher.

1 2 3 4 5 6 7 8 9 0 DOC/DOC 0 1 0 9

ISBN 978-0-07-162960-7
MHID 0-07-162960-2

McGraw-Hill books are available at special quantity discounts to use as premiums and sales promotions, or for use in corporate training programs. To contact a representative please e-mail us at bulksales@mcgraw-hill.com.

This book is printed on recycled, acid-free paper.

Library of Congress Cataloging-in-Publication Data
Smith, Jon, 1975-
  Be #1 on Google : 52 fast and easy search engine optimization tools to drive customers to your web site / by Jon Smith.
    p. cm.
  ISBN 0-07-162960-2 (alk. paper)
  1. Google. 2. Internet marketing. 3. Internet searching. 4. Web search engines. I. Title.
II. Title: Be number one on Google.
  HF5415.1265.S6144 2010
  658.8'72—dc22   2009011280

Contents

Contents

Careful Now

There are both good and bad sources of information available on the Internet and in the telephone directory and advertised on bad photocopies for 20 cents a week at the local newsstand. The Internet especially is a constantly changing phenomenon, and therefore good and bad sites are forever popping up and dropping off. Web addresses change, so if a link doesn't work, be sure to use Google to try to find a site's new home or a similar service offered by another firm or individual. Likewise, you should have an up-to-date virus checker installed before you visit new sites and download anything at all. You also should be aware that new applications may squabble and bicker over who's the daddy—they may not work because of the other things you have installed on your machine. We're sorry about all this and wish it were a better world, but it's the only one we have. We believe in taking it on the chin like grown-ups and expect you to do the same thing. We love you dearly, but if it all goes wrong, you're on your own; we assume no liability. See it as an adventure.

Introduction

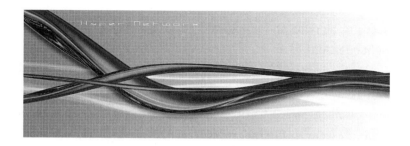

There's having a Web site and there's having a Web site that works. It's all very well to have a flashy intro, a fully integrated shopping basket, and lots of features and functionality that can wow the audience on every single page. But what if they can't find you? What if you're not visible on the search engines and on Google in particular? If they don't know your address (which most users don't), many members of your potential audience are going to try to find your site by typing in a keyword or phrase, and if you don't rank on those return results, you may as well not have a Web site at all. It's that serious.

Making your site Google-friendly or employing Search Engine Optimization techniques, or SEO, as it's known in the trade, at your earliest convenience should be a priority; SEO is this year's black. What it can cost varies wildly, so be sure to question the worth of both the cheapest and the most expensive service providers, but remember that there's lots that can be done internally and at minimal cost other than your time. This book will show you what needs to be done and empower you to ask your SEO service provider—and yourself—the right questions.

To ignore Search Engine Optimization (and Google in particular) is folly. Having your own Web site means you simply must get involved with SEO techniques. Without any SEO input, well, if I were a betting man (which I'm not), I'd say your chances of success were about even; if I were an Internet project manager (which I am), I would say you were dead in the water. Your site is nothing if it isn't optimized for the Web. In fact, ignoring SEO is tantamount to placing a brick wall against the front door of a high-end shop: You're actually blocking your users from reaching you. You're destined to become part of the noise of the Internet rather than a music maker. You're streaming without a paddle.

So how do you use this book? Dip in and dip out, read it from start to finish—it really doesn't matter. The 52 brilliant ideas contained in it are generally quick fixes that should result in immediate benefits to your site if you adopt them. If your budget is modest, implementing just a handful of these ideas will improve your Web site rankings and help you realize your ambitions and the ambitions of your company. Employ all 52 and people will be throwing themselves down on the floor and proposing—no, wait, I mean finding your Web site, buying more of your products, reading your information, and coming back to your site again and again.

 # Idea 1

What's So Special about Google, Then?
Is It Really All That?

Google this and Google that! What about Yahoo, AltaVista, and all those other search engines? My mom always said, "Don't put all your eggs in one basket."

Say It with Numbers

When Internet users are unable or unwilling to guess your URL (Uniform Resource Locator; read "Web site address"), they will use a search engine to find you. Now, among all the Web site visits that are conducted in the United States that were immediately preceded by a search engine search, Google is responsible for the majority. Google is by far the most widely used search engine and the biggest referrer of visitors in the United States (60 percent of all searches).*

Google, like Kleenex, has achieved a dominance so great, in such a short period of time, that the company name often is used to mean Internet searching. Single execs, looking for companionship, "google" potential dates before committing to a meal. Parents google a school

* Hitwise Search Results (December 2005) www.hitwise.com.

to decide whether it's suitable for little Frankie's education. Job applicants google the interview staff to learn any interesting snippets that they can bring up at an interview (and vice versa). Internet users use Google—a lot.

Google, certainly at the moment, owns the Internet, and if you want your online business to thrive, you need to learn how to be #1 on Google.

Just Flick the Switch?

As an e-business adviser and freelance e-consultant I meet with a lot of companies with Web sites. Primarily they all want the same thing—good exposure on Google. But there is no magic switch, there is no instant cure; becoming #1 on Google takes time. You want instant gratification, and Google's more interested in pursuing a long-term relationship with you. This may

go against everything else we see, hear, and feel about the Web (overnight success stories, sites plucked from obscurity, servers crashing under the weight of so much traffic . . .), but that's the deal. Commit seriously to Google and it will commit right back, and when that relationship is forged, it's not just strong, it's *really* strong.

Sleeping with the Enemy

Unfortunately, Google doesn't make it easy. You'd think the easiest thing in the world would be for Google to post an FAQ page or a checklist on the site that systematically explained to developers and business owners how to win its favor, but it won't. Why? Well, basically, Google is fed up with people abusing the system, and if there's no obvious system, that makes said abuse that much harder. And it works. So is there an official Google-endorsed guide to Google? No, only unofficial guides, and this is one of them.

Here's an Idea for You . . .

Let's see where you are right now. Type in your domain name on a Google search (without the www and the .com). Are you on page 1, page 2, page 3? Now type in the name of your best-selling product, service, or industry. Are you on page 1, page 2, page 3? Okay, there are plenty of ideas for you to improve that listing and get you not just to the top of the page for each of those searches but filling page 1 completely, with separate links to areas of your site.

Idea 2

I Wanna Be Number 1
Taking the Restricted View

No matter which search term I choose, my competitor is always number 1 and I'm not even on the first page. How can I compete?

The Smaller Picture

Whatever industry or service your Web site offers, it's fair to say that you are part of a very busy marketplace. You're not the first Web site, nor will you be the last. Understanding and, more important, accepting that you are not the only player is a major stepping-stone to ensuring that you will be successful. I'm serious. No idea is original, and deciding to use the Web as your sales outlet is certainly not groundbreaking—someone, somewhere has been doing it successfully or unsuccessfully far longer than you, and many more will follow. But don't let that put you off.

Keyword Ego

There are top-level keywords in every industry. As an online toy seller, I was obsessed with the keyword "toys," but it quickly became apparent that I was up against Toys 'R' Us; yet we were in a different market, and in terms of long-term marketing spend we simply couldn't compete. The click-throughs we got for paying for the keyword "toys" weren't converting into sales. What was the matter? The answer was that we had a specialist offering: traditional-style wooden toys, finger puppets, stroller toys, and off-the-wall clothing and footwear. The simple fact is that people who typed in the word "toys" were looking for the latest craze, invariably made of plastic, which had enjoyed advertising on television. That wasn't the sort of stuff we sold. Okay, we sold toys, but not the "toys" these people were looking for.

The answer: Go niche. Be specific. We optimized our site on the specific, not the generic—"wooden toys," "push-along toys," and the like—and the results were staggering. Suddenly we were enjoying more traffic and, more important, a higher conversion ratio. In simple terms we were attracting the right sort of customer who was interested in our offering, and more of those customers were committing to purchase.

Special and Unique

Your potential customers are both of these things: special in that they require extra attention and unique in that they really do think for themselves. We are all guilty of forcing Web users into a certain category, but the truth is, they're as different and picky about their Web habits as they are about their everyday decisions. Treat them as individuals.

Here's an Idea for You . . .

In your opinion, right now, what are the top three keywords that you think are important to your site? Got them? Right, forget about them. They're not important (for now). Now create a list of 10 keywords that are the next most important in the list (as far as you're concerned). These are the niche words, the important words; these words will make you rich. Write these words down. We'll use them and turn that process into revenue; I promise.

Idea 3

It's Not Yogurt . . .
Organic (or Natural) versus Paid-For

Whatever your views about "good" bacteria are, there is a huge distinction to be made between healthy listings and unhealthy ones.

Thirty-three percent of Internet users perceive a company in the top search engine rankings to be a major brand.*

Pay for It, You Will

I'm not against paid-for listings, not at all. A good AdWords campaign can and will bring profit to a Web site that exploits that offering well. But before we go down the route of paid-for placement, we need to do everything we can to ensure that your site is search-engine-friendly and ranking well, without committing to a financial outlay—and at the end of the day, AdWords is always going to cost you money, especially in the short term. Have a campaign but

*iProspect search engine branding survey: www.iprospect.com.

make sure you are maximizing your site to perform well in the natural or organic listings also.

Your target should be to rank high naturally *and* be featured within the AdWords listings because two listings on page 1 of Google are always going to look stronger than a single one.

They're Just So Switched on Nowadays

The average Internet user is getting clever. These users are becoming wise to the fact that the search results at the top of the page and on the right-hand side are there only because someone is paying for the privilege. Therefore, many people will actively *not* click through them, preferring to explore the natural search results—the sites that are there because of their SEO and content merits, not their marketing spend. You must ensure that you are ranking there too.

Here's an Idea for You . . .

To get a feel for the disparity and similarities of how Web sites perform in the paid-for and natural listings, make a few searches on Google. Try "posters," "auction," and "toys." Notice any patterns? Are there some companies you would have thought would be paying for placement that aren't? Now do a specific search for your industry. Do you appear on the first page? Who are your competitors? Do they have a good natural listing and/or a paid-for placement? By understanding what others are doing within your market you will quickly ascertain what you need to be doing to compete effectively.

Idea 4

View Askew
How Google Sees Your Site

> I wanna become the name everyone thinks of when vacuum cleaners are mentioned.... Set realistic goals, strive for them, and enjoy the results.

Aspiring to be number 1 on Google only exposes the public's general disregard and the false understanding most business owners have for Google and for search engines in general.

Your major qualifying interest—your cash cows, i.e., your paying customers—aren't the random surfers who type in "toys" or "books" or "flowers." It's far more specific and targeted than that. Your (and my) customers are after a particular item or service—the long tail, if you will—right here, right now. Although branding is very important, if I need a hand-tied bouquet delivered by 10 a.m. tomorrow, I don't care who gets the business, as long as they deliver. And that's true across the board.

View Askew—Google's Take

Joe Public wants to be number 1—I do, you do, your competitor does . . . the list continues. It's quite obvious that we can't all be number 1, so how does it work? Web users are becoming ever more advanced; if they are looking for that hand-tied bouquet, that's exactly what they will type in as their search term; they might even add a location. So if you're a florist in Manhattan, you'd be far better optimizing your site to become number 1 for "bouquet Manhattan" or "funeral flowers Manhattan" than you would trying to make an impact with the keyword "flowers."

Your Battle Plan

What phrases are your customers using to find you? What phrases *should* be leading them to you? And what can you do to capitalize on this? The simple answer is to find out which words and phrases Internet

users are really using in any given month and capitalizing on that information. Google offers a similar tool if you're signed up for its AdWords program, but if you're not, Yahoo offers something just as powerful (the only difference being that if you want a truer indication of a search term and its popularity, including Google, you're going to have to multiply the figures they quote by five).

Here's an Idea for You . . .

Go to the Web site http://sem.smallbusiness.yahoo.com/searchenginemarketing/—this is Yahoo's Keyword Assistant. Type in the keyword you are interested in tracking. The clever thing about Keyword Assistant is that it also returns related results; this means that a single search can return a lot of serious data about the keywords you were interested in exploiting and, often, keywords you weren't. In a matter of minutes you'll be able to see where you're going wrong, what needs to be added to your meta information and your body text, and a clear indication of whether you need to be creating multiple sites on the Web.

Idea 5

Uncovering the Data
Unleashing Your Inner Miss Marple

Research is critical to any business: What are your competitors doing? What is the market doing? Dust off that magnifying glass, start wearing tweed, and let's find out.

Yahoo offers a keyword checker, but what else can you use to find out more? Well, there are a selection of sites offering business-critical information about keywords; some you pay for, some you don't. I'm going to concentrate on the free information because it's strong and accurate, and if you are happy to invest the time, why pay someone else?

www.wordtracker.com

We might think we know what keywords people often use and think we know how many competitors are out there, but Wordtracker will be able to tell you categorically if we are correct in our assumptions. Go to the site and enter the keywords or phrases you are interested in. The great thing about Wordtracker is that it also will show you how many users searched for that word today and what the competition is like for your selected keyword or phrase—and give the results a numerical score, known as a KEI or keyword effectiveness index, so that you will know instantly whether you are one of few or one of many competing for a keyword. If you're lucky, there will be some words or phrases with a KEI of more than 300, which means a word is a popular keyword with very little competition; any score of more than 50 is well worth optimizing. You should focus your marketing attention on these words.

www.nichebot.com

This is a really handy tool, and it's free. Nichebot takes its data from both Yahoo and Wordtracker; it then merges the information and displays the results accordingly. Nichebot uses its own algorithm to display the data, and a good score on Nichebot is a very low number, as opposed to the opposite system used by Wordtracker.

I think Nichebot is handy if you're short on time, but I've noticed discrepancies between the data provided on Nichebot and the data you can get from its sources (Yahoo and Wordtracker). Therefore, I would run the tests separately if time allowed.

Here's an Idea for You . . .

Don't just add these Web addresses to your favorites or promise yourself that you'll take a look in a few days—do it right now. This data is accurate only up to the date of the search. A single look at the data won't allow for peaks and valleys. What you need to be doing is collecting and collating this information, and you should continue to do that over the coming weeks. Create a spreadsheet with the most important keywords and the associated number of searches—are there patterns, trends, or fluctuations that might have an impact on your business over a 12-month period?

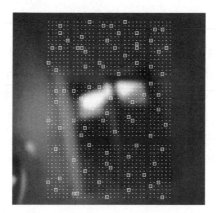

 Idea 6

Pimp My Metadata
The Hidden Message

Your message to the search engines often is hidden within the code that makes up the site. It may be out of sight, but it's no less important. Here's how to pimp it up.

Title

Of all the information you can include in the header of your site, your title is by far the one that's most appreciated and regarded by Google. It dictates the bit of text that appears right at the top of the page of your own or your user's Web browser, and it provides confirmation that the users have arrived at the correct destination and your site has what they want. For example, if I had a site selling rare stamps I'd want the title to reflect something along the lines of "rare and hard-to-find stamps, for serious collectors—24-hour delivery."

Meta Keywords

Your keywords are the words under which you feel your Web site should be ranked. For instance, if you sell skateboards and related products, your home page keywords should include the words skaters will be interested in:

> <META name="keywords" content="skate shoes, footwear, skateboarding, Heelys, skateboards, inline skates, skate clothing, hoodies, t-shirts, tees, jeans">

The classic problem most Web sites have is coming up with a great list of keywords and then repeating them on every single page. No! Keep it specific. Use a keyword (or for that matter a reference in your title or description) only if that word is used in the page within the body text—if you do not, you'll be penalized.

My developer said that Google doesn't pay any attention to keywords anymore—and that is right; it doesn't. But although this is about Google, I'm not blinded by loyalty enough to ignore the other search engines out there that do pay attention to meta keywords—in fact, that's a whopping 20 percent of the search market, constituting one in five of your potential customers. Not to be sniffed at or ignored. Put it like this: The day Amazon stops using meta keywords is the day I'll stop; these people spend millions researching the Web.

Meta Description

So someone does a Google search and is presented with about 12 results per page. That person sees a long list of Web addresses and a bit of introductory text about the site . . . where do you think that text comes from? Well, if you don't include a meta description, it will be chosen randomly from a page on your site and, quite frankly, might not make an awful lot of sense. Alternatively, you can add a meta description, which is a one- or two-sentence description of your Web site. This should also be a sales message to potential visitors—what's going to make them click on your link and not a competitor's? Strong, clean copy is the answer: a sales message, a teaser, a call to action to encourage them to click through to you.

Here's an Idea for You . . .

Write a one-sentence descriptive comment that describes what information and products users will find on your home page. This will become your title. Once you're happy with that, personalize it a bit, and the result will become your meta description. But don't stop there. You've only answered the problem of the home page; now you need to repeat the process for every single page on your site. Remember that less is more and be specific.

Idea 7

That Keyword Is So Owned
Satellite Sites

If you have an engineering Web site and the company name is ABC Inc., is your best course of action to rely on www.abcinc.com? Well, no, not really.

Guerrilla Marketing

With the best will in the world, calling your Web site by your company name may seem the most normal and natural course of action . . . and it's certainly worth buying the domain just to protect yourself. However, to truly sell and market yourself through the Internet, you need to understand how Web users operate and how they are likely to find you.

I spend my days teaching Web site owners how to improve their sites and how to get them noticed. This week, for example, I met with a client who offers training courses to managers of businesses who is based in Hampshire in the United Kingdom. He'd been operating his business using a Web site domain name similar to www.abcltd.com, which was fine but was doing him no favors in terms of attracting new customers unfamiliar with his company. A quick search on the Web (I used www.123-reg.co.uk) revealed that at the time of writing, the following domain names were available:

www.leadership-management-training.net—available from $18 for 2 years
www.management-training.gb.com—available from $30 for 2 years
www.management-training-hampshire.co.uk—available from $6 for 2 years
www.management-training-hampshire.com—available from $18 for 2 years
www.management-skills-training.co.uk—available from $6 for 2 years
www.business-management-training.net—available from $18 for 2 years

All keyword-heavy, available, and cheap!

Case Study

I once had a Web site called www.toytopia.co.uk (query Google even now and it's flooded with references to a company that ceased trading four years ago). Although the Toytopia site did very well in terms of traffic and customers, we noticed that some of the items we sold were being featured on TV and in the Sunday newspaper supplements. That had nothing to do with us, but we were obviously selling items that really appealed to an audience and wanted to capitalize on this free PR. A quick search of our bestsellers revealed that wheeliebugs were a major cash cow for us, and within weeks we launched www.wheeliebugs.co.uk, which was a dedicated site specifically for wheeliebugs. This product was being featured in a magazine or a news item every week; all we did was provide a sales outlet based on the keywords that people would remember—in this case, the actual name of the product: "wheeliebugs." Although the Toytopia site ranked highly on a wheeliebugs search, nothing is stronger than owning the very domain name itself: the keywords that encapsulate the product or the theme. The site rocked and became a business in its own right. It cost us $3 for the domain name for 12 months and $200 to transfer aspects of the site across and netted us almost $140,000.

A Word of Warning

If you buy keyword-heavy domains, be sure to set up small (even single-page) Web sites at each address rather than opting for the simple redirect option—Google really doesn't like this and may unleash its fury. It's better to have a keyword-heavy site (even though it's only one page) with a link through to your main site than to force users across by using a redirect. Theoretically, if you get your SEO right, you'll have a couple of listings on page 1 of Google's search results made up of the main site and the satellite sites, thus forcing your competitors' sites farther and farther down in the listings.

Here's an Idea for You . . .

Using a variety of search tools, find out what keywords are being used and the number of people searching in any given month or day. Does this sort of traffic seem attractive? Would 1 percent or 2 percent of those people make a huge difference to your business? If so, it's time to start setting up satellite Web sites to capture as much search traffic as possible.

Idea 8

Analyze This
Google Analytics

Without knowing how you're performing now, you have no way of knowing if any of your changes make a bit of difference.

The Sign-Up

Google Analytics is a popular service, so popular, in fact, that it can take a few weeks for you to be approved after signing up. Bear this in mind and start the sign-up process as soon as you can. Once you are approved, you will be given a small bit of code, which will need to be added to every page of your site that you want to track—for most of us, that means every page. Your user name and password will give you access to a host of statistics regarding your site.

In a Nutshell

So what's it all about? Well, Analytics is a great way to check visually what's going on in terms of traffic on your site—how many people are visiting, what they're looking at, how long they stay, and the city or town from where they are visiting. Not bad for free. With these data you are then able to set targets and goals for the performance of the site, and the data are collected and presented to you through an easy-to-use graphical interface. If you are using or plan to use paid-for ads through Google (AdWords), it makes sense to sign up as the two programs are so interrelated and in a way interdependent.

Other Benefits?

Again, Google makes no mention of it, but I can't help feeling that having some Google code on your site is a pretty good indication of how important you feel Google is to the site. Therefore, I can't help feeling that—unofficially—your loyalty and acceptance of Google do not go unnoticed and unrewarded in terms of how often your site is visited by the Googlebot and how it is subsequently ranked.

Its Word Is Law . . .

Actually it's not, and at the end of the day Google is a business looking to make a profit, so although at the moment the Analytics program works really well, it should always be used in conjunction with your own stats package (usually standard with most Web sites these days). It is interesting to compare and contrast the data from both sources—they should, of course, be telling you the same thing, but that is not always the case.

Here's an Idea for You . . .

Pop over to www.google.com/analytics and sign up. Once you receive approval, add (or have your developer add) the "urchin" code to your Web pages, and within 24 hours you'll be receiving accurate data about activity on your site. (Repeat the process for each and every domain name/site you own.) You can track as many separate domains through one Analytics account as you wish.

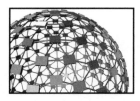

Idea 9

Destination Me
The Importance of Inbound Links

Once it worked like this: I've got a Web site, you've got a Web site, let's reciprocally link. Nowadays this won't help either of you. The rules most definitely have changed!

Inbound Is King

People abused the system, and now we're all being punished. I no longer refer to a friend's or a favored business contact's Web site on my site unless it has a direct relevance to the content of my site. Gone are the days when you'd click on a "links" page and see a cornucopia of interesting, sassy, and amusing sites—why? Well, if a site is still playing this game, it is likely to be penalized. Therefore, it's in the site owner's best interest to remove all links that don't positively affect his or her own rankings. That means getting rid of the chaff and actively seeking and encouraging the great and the good. So who are the good?

25 ▶

PageRank

There is some confusion over this name. Although in effect it means the rank of your Web page or Web site, the actual name derives from Larry Page, one of Google's founders. He created an algorithm to assign a numerical value to a Web site or page— 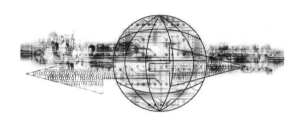 essentially designed to promote relevance, authority, and clear meaning. This numerical value (expressed as a figure between 0 and 10) reflects the popularity of a Web site; it incorporates a number of defining factors, but let's concentrate on the relevance of links here.

What about Outbound?

This certainly shouldn't be your focus, but making your site search-engine-friendly and offering your users something value-added and providing a service is important. If you are selling

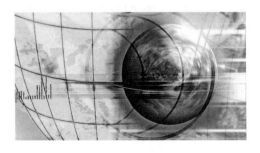

a product and feel that adding a link to the manufacturer or a fan site or any other site will benefit your business, your quest to make your site search-engine-friendly shouldn't become a neurotic obsession. Include the link; your primary customer is your human users, not the Googlebot. Remaining search-engine-friendly is, of course, important—but if you can enrich the life of your users and help them feel comfortable with the information you provide, they're more likely to buy your product or service or link to you. This is what will make your Web site a success, not Google.

Here's an Idea for You . . .

Download the Google Toolbar from www.google.com/tools/firefox/toolbar, and if you're not using Firefox as your Web browser, simply type "Google Toolbar" into Google. It will reply with the correct URL, depending on your browser. The Google Toolbar will offer you a number of tools but, most important, will display the PageRank of any page you are visiting. Examples of sites with a high PageRank are www.bbc.com and www.google.com (no surprise there!). For a hard-core explanation of the mathematics and algorithm behind Google's PageRank, check out this listing on Wikipedia: http://en.wikipedia.org/wiki/PageRank.

Idea 10

Who's Lookin'?
Keyword Bias

Research suggests that only 7 percent of Web sites employ any search engine optimization whatsoever. Get this right and you're on your way to fame and fortune.

Finding key phrases to attract potential customers is critical. Most businesses that decide to trade on the Internet establish themselves offline first. They have created a brand and try to replicate that brand online. But a brand is nontransferable as is. You have to work on building both an offline and an online presence.

Far Too Specific, or Not . . .

If you ask Marlene, who owns the domain name www.marlenescakes.co.uk, where she ranks on Google.co.uk, chances are, she'll say number 1. But she'll be referring to searches conducted containing the keywords "marlene" and "cakes"—and that is not how people search. No one knows Marlene, so, when in need of some cake, they will search for "cake" or "wedding cake" or "birthday cake, San Francisco." As far as the search engines are concerned, Marlene and her site do not exist because she hasn't optimized her site to this level. Users will be directed to the sites that have capitalized on the generic search terms (or keywords), and the site that appears in the search results will gain the customers even though, theoretically, the company might be on the other side of the world. Marlene may well have the most appropriate offering, but if users can't find her, her site may as well not be there.

Finding the Most Appropriate Key Phrases

It's all very well having a sexy business name such as Orion Services, but the name itself means nothing. Are you a scientific agency dealing with the mapping of the stars, a washing-machine repairer, or a business consultancy? Who knows? Your potential customer certainly doesn't know, and no amount of searching on Google is likely to find you. Your domain name should incorporate

your key deliverables. If you're a guesthouse on Martha's Vineyard, include some of those terms in your domain name. I used to sell wooden toys online, and the business was called Toytopia—a clever name simply because it incorporated the keyword that defined the product. If you provide management training it's no good calling yourself Atlantis Inc.; far better to be Management-Trainer.com. These are the sorts of phrases Internet users employ, so work this to your advantage.

Here's an Idea for You . . .

Within your Web browser, open your Web site and view its source code to see your own meta keywords (in some versions of Internet Explorer, for example, you do this by clicking on "view" and then "source"). Use the same technique to view your competitors' pages and those of any other Web sites that interest you. Chances are, you'll soon learn what works and what doesn't. You'll see what techniques your competitors are employing and what can be copied across to your site—and all this critical information is available for free!

# Idea 11

Who Are Ya?
It's All in the Details, So Does Your Domain Registration Tally?

Is what you say about yourself true? Is it still the case? People (and Google) can check—so what does your WHOIS record say about you?

Inadvertent Mistake

When many people set up a Web site, the idea—or even the company—is still to be fully created. This is normal and not a problem. When you are buying the domain name (or instructing others to buy it on your behalf), you personally quote your home address as the contact. You register yourself as "nontrading" because, right now, you're not trading.

However, over time the business is launched and the WHOIS details remain the same—you may be employing a staff of 15 and turning over a couple of million dollars, but your WHOIS record implies that you are a one-man band operating out of a garage. Most users won't notice, but some might—especially customers who might want to do business with you, such as running a joint venture or a copromotion or even becoming a buyer of your business. More important, Google can see. Again, there's no specific mention, but if you're running a

.com business from the United Kingdom (or, conversely, a .co.uk business from outside the United Kingdom), this shows up in terms of where the server is hosted, the physical contact address you've quoted, and the contact e-mail address. Keep it local for the market you want to appeal to.

You can run a WHOIS report from numerous Web sites. For starters, try www.whois.net and check that everything is present and correct. If your Web site developers accidentally have put their address as the registrant, have this changed. For .co.uk addresses, contact Nominet at www.nominet.org.uk

Staying in Control

Although your service provider probably will e-mail you many months in advance of the expiration of your domain name, what if it forgets? Or goes out of business? Or deliberately doesn't tell you because another one of its clients is interested in the domain? It's your responsibility to reregister your domain names, not anyone else's. Use WHOIS to determine when the expiration date is and then set a reminder in your diary or online calendar one month beforehand so that you can check that it has been taken care of. There's nothing harder than trying to regain control of a domain that has expired—in fact, it's far easier for a complete stranger to come along and buy it from under your nose.

Here's an Idea for You . . .

Make sure your WHOIS information reflects you and your business in the best possible light. There's nothing wrong with working from home (I do it too) but make the first line of the address look like a business: "Company House, 14 Elm Street. . . ." Yes, it's nonsense, but it works, and if I was interested in talking to you at a commercial level, I'd have a very different view of a business that has its own premises as opposed to one apparently trading from a residential address. As far as Google is concerned, a UK address for a .co.uk domain name is always going to look more legitimate than a foreign one or a PO box number. And of course, in the United States, you just have .com.

Idea 12

Open with a Joke
Keyword Prominence and Relevance

Google, for all its head-of-the-table bravado, likes a snappy, sassy introduction to a Web site—no idealistic diatribe, just the truth in bite-sized pieces.

Less Is More, Baby . . .

Although there are some complicated algorithms at play (which are constantly changing), a page that will work successfully on Google is a page that is created simply and follows this basic premise. When you (or your developer) are creating a Web page, the top 25 percent of the page and the very bottom of the page are the most important parts. This is not to say that everything in between is ignored—far from it—but Google wants to see prominence given to the critical or key words and phrases by which you are looking to be ranked.

Don't, therefore, waste the prime real estate or the top of a page on a lengthy introduction to the site or the topic but get right in there—go straight for the jugular and be conscious of the prominence and relevance you give to the keywords being quoted. If you sell trendy T-shirts, you need to be dropping in the brands you carry, not a monologue about the importance of T-shirts or a history of the garment. Start selling product both to the user and to Google. Let them all know that you mean business.

The very bottom of the page is equally as important. Does your page taper off with a couple of halfhearted links to the privacy policy and a copyright statement? Or does it include the pertinent navigational options repeated as text-only links that will add both to the user's ability to continue navigating your site and to Google's ability to notice yet another reference to a certain type of T-shirt, thus helping you to rise up in the rankings because of relevance and prominence?

H Tags

The jury's out about the weighting of H tags, but I remain convinced that as long as you don't try to abuse the system (by tagging every subject as H1), considering all other factors, they work. H tags are the way you tell the search engines that this "H" (header) is worth paying attention to. **It's like making a sentence bold**; it gets noticed. Though you may have altered the text physically to be bold or italic or presented it in a larger font, Google ignores this because it's cosmetic. It's looking for H tags, and your job is to list them in order of relevance.

If there are four main foci to your Web page, you're well within your rights to label each one with an H tag, ideally listed in rank order—H1, H2, H3, and so on. Though labeling each topic H1 might win you a short-term gain, it's foolhardy and eventually will be penalized. Equally, if there's only one major topic or point to the page, add your H1 tag but don't be tempted to add others for no real reason.

Here's an Idea for You . . .

If you have not employed H tags yet, reassess your Web pages and assign those tags to the pertinent points on each page. If you already are using H tags, check that they are being utilized correctly. Are they relevant? Do they add to the site? Will they help or hinder the site in terms of being ranked? If there are any more than six on a page, ditch the overkill.

 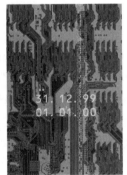 

Idea 13

Laid-Back Surfers
The Google Search

Google has made us all lazy: You want to find a site, you search. You want to find something on a particular Web site, you search. So do you offer search?

Seek and Ye Shall Find

When users first visit a Web site, they have no idea whether there are ten pages or 10,000 pages behind the site—and sometimes, in our cash-rich, time-poor lifestyles, we don't even have a few seconds to spare to find out. You might have spent hours agonizing over the clever navigation and categories that define your site; it might actually be quite good. But there are navigators and there are searchers, and behavioral profiling suggests that the latter are becoming the norm. Therefore, if users visit your site after following a link from Google, they will want instant gratification—the answer on a plate. Can you offer them what they want and need? It's all very well for you to know that within three clicks they can explore the depth and breadth of your entire product catalogue, but that's a massive 20 seconds of time and thought—which many Web users will not give you. A search tool is the answer and is something you should give high priority to implementing.

In Bed with Google, Again . . .

It's that old way of thinking yet again, but common sense will tell you that if you can't afford to install an integrated search tool on your own site, the Google Search is the only alternative. They are not going to ignore or punish a site that has included Google code within the HTML—this is mutual back-scratching at its best. Offer your users a chance to search your site; they'll love you for it. You can download Enterprise Solutions from www.google.com/enterprise/ enterprise_search.html.

Here's an Idea for You . . .

Visit all of your competitors' sites and pay particular attention to their search tools; if they don't have one, note that. Now, what do you like about their search and what doesn't work? Search for both obvious industry-specific terms and the more obscure ones. What's coming back—helpful, pertinent results? Nothing? Irrelevant results? Or, worse, the wrong results? Now that you are armed with the knowledge of where they are going wrong, it's time to invest in your own search tool or use Google's. Despite its flaws, it will prove very useful in the short term while you are busy creating your own.

Idea 14

Selling Out
Accepting Google Advertising

It may be that over 90 percent of your visitors don't order from you or contact you ... so you might as well try to make some money from them another way.

Losing Customers

Yes, the price you pay for offering any form of linked advertising on your site is that you effectively are sending traffic away from your site—but you are getting paid for it. If your site is a portal or an information site, advertising will be one of your major revenue streams.

Google versus Specific Advertisers

The problem for most small or newer sites is that they don't have a huge amount of traffic, and established advertisers aren't going to want to work with them until they can prove that they have big numbers. Google isn't fussy; it will work with everyone and anyone. If you want to start earning money from your site immediately, join the AdSense program. Again, there's no proof of this on the Google site, but another bit of Google code on your site has to make the Googlebot more favorable toward it—expect more visits and a higher ranking.

Make Money from Your Site

It's true: At 2 a.m. someone, somewhere might be interested in buying something. That someone might be looking for the very thing that you sell via an affiliate. That item might be a book that retails at $10.99, and your commission might be 10 percent. You might ask, Is it worth it for $1.09? Well, as a single sale, probably not. But what if you have a targeted audience visiting your site and buying products via your affiliate deals? Suddenly that $1.09 is repeated again and again and

becomes more and more and more. To sign up to AdSense, go to https://www.google.com/ adsense/login/en_GB/?hl=en_GB.

I would consider this option only if you have enough traffic to make this process worthwhile. The financial reward must compensate for the dilution of your own brand/site and the fact that you are sending potential customers away.

Here's an Idea for You . . .

Join AdSense, and once your account has been created, add a link on a page of your site. Not on your home page but maybe on a page that is not part of your core offering or one that needs a little more content that you haven't gotten around to writing yet. See if AdSense works for you. Are customers clicking on it? Are the revenues pretty good? Would they be even better if you added the campaign across the entire site? Give it a try and see what happens.

Idea 15

Say That Again?
Keyword Proximity

The art of good text on a Web site is not flowery prose and poetic sentiment—it's all about shouting about what's on offer.

This means what the user (and Google) can find on your page and answering this very basic question: Do you sell or provide the information or product I am looking for? If you can answer this in your first paragraph, you're well on your way to being a successful site.

Writing Like a Pro

It's all very well having world-beating content on your site, but is it in the right place? Web pages can be very long; sometimes this is good and sometimes it's bad, but don't be too concerned with length of the text. Instead, focus your attention on where on the page the keywords and phrases you've chosen appear. Are they being used in the most effective way possible?

We've seen that Google favors keywords and phrases that appear right at the top of the

page, and therein lies the key. This isn't a novel or a play that you're writing. We don't need a gentle fluffy introduction to what's going on; we don't need to be warmed up. You need to come out with all guns blazing, with a definitive statement that summarizes what is contained on that page. It should be rich in keywords and phrases, direct, clear, and constantly calling the user to action. Use the rest of the text to explain and qualify your statements, not the other way around.

Good "Spider Food"

Although it is the human user you ultimately must appeal to if the Web site itself is going to be effective, the Googlebot and other search engine spiders also must be at the forefront of your mind when you are creating copy for your Web pages. This all boils down to a neat little marriage that will keep both parties interested and happy, and it's known as keyword density. If you flood your text with keywords, it won't make sense to your end users and will lead them to abandon the site. Therefore, you should be looking for a density of about 4 percent, which means that for every hundred words of text on your page, you should mention your keyword four times. Stick with this rule and the spiders, the bots, the crawlers, and even the human users will regard your content as strong.

Here's an Idea for You . . .

Pick a product page or a page that describes one of your services and take a long hard look at the text. Have you mentioned everything, at least once, that was hinted at in the meta data? Have you placed the most important keywords and phrases (including brands) within the first and second paragraphs of the text? Can the user and Google click on some or all of these keywords to learn more? If that is not the case, start reworking the text so that it appeals to both the human user and Google. Yes, you will need to compromise, but this is business, not a creative writing course.

# Idea 16

Jargon Busting
Hits, Visitors, Page Views, and Uniques . . .

As with all industries, the world of Web sites is peppered with its own lingo. Get to know it well and nobody will be able to pull the wool over your avatar.

Hits

This is the most abused and wrongly used statistic referring to Web activity. You've heard people say, "I get 100,000 hits a month." Meaningless. A hit refers to each file sent by the server to a Web browser—therefore, if you have a page that contains seven images, chances are that those images plus the HTML file supporting them will register as eight hits. The numbers quickly get out of hand, and you have no real idea how many visitors your site is getting.

Page Views

Page views are a more accurate measure, because the figure disregards how many hits or files make up the Web page. It simply measures how many times a Web page was served up. The problem with page views is that you don't know whether it was one user looking at 20 pages or 20 visitors looking at one page each.

Visitors/Uniques

This should be the number you are paying the most attention to. This is the truest representation of how popular your site is. More accurate than hits or page views, your visitor numbers show how many people actually came to your site.

PPC

Price per click is the financial reward someone will pay you for every click he or she receives from an advert placed on your site—or the price you pay Google, for example, every time someone clicks on your AdWords advert. Clients often ask what a good PPC rate is, and the answer is that it depends. It's worth only what someone is prepared to pay.

PPM

This is less and less common nowadays, but some advertisers don't want to mess around with a micropayment for every single click-through. They're looking at this relationship in the macro sense and expect you to be sending over loads of visitors. They therefore prefer to work in terms of thousands of visitors rather than anything smaller. The letter "M" is the Latin representation of 1,000, and thus PPM is the price per thousand.

Here's an Idea for You . . .

I'm assuming that you've already signed up with Google Analytics and the information is flooding through, but don't rely only on these statistics; get a second opinion. Maybe your developer has bolted a Web site statistics function onto your site, but if that is not the case, check out www.opentracker.com, which is a great tool for measuring activity. If you're considering marketing your site on search engines other than Google, it is essential.

Idea 17

Here, Look Over Here
Registering with Search Engines

Google and the other search engines are good—but they're not omnipotent. Let them know you've arrived on the scene; be bold, be noticed, and be listed.

Lost in the Noise

There are literally millions of new Web sites and Web pages being added to the Internet every day. Google is trying to keep up but likes us to flag a major change or a new development. Launching a site and expecting to be found by search engines and customers alike is just not going to work. You need to leave a trail of bread crumbs and, better yet, set off an unmistakable fanfare to announce your arrival. Manually submit your Web address to the major search engines to get the ball rolling.

Google: http://www.google.com/addurl

If you're feeling lazy, type "Add URL" into Google and you'll see the link you need. Google offers a host of Webmaster tools that are worth investigating, but for now fill in the blanks and submit. Expect a visit from the Googlebot within about three weeks.

Yahoo: http://search.yahoo.com/info/submit.html

This is not as slick as the Google Web address and you have to register with Yahoo to use the page, but it's worth it and is recommended.

AltaVista: http://addurl.altavista.com/addurl/default

Lycos: www.lycos.co.uk/inc/foot/addasite.html

If you fancy jump-starting your appearance on any other search engines, just search for "submit URL" on your search engine of choice. Be sure that you submit yourself only once in any given month as the search engines see repeated listing requests as spam; check whether your developer has done it first. Have one member of your staff responsible for submitting to all the engines.

Paying the Hired Help

Avoid the many hundreds of sites that offer to submit your site to all the major search engines on your behalf—they want money from you for what is a simple exercise. Also, you can't be sure it's been done and won't know if they've done it correctly. Finally, most of the submission pages ask you to copy the wavy security text they provide so that they can determine whether the "submit URL" request has been generated by a human user or by software—you can bet your bottom server that they will pay more attention to the requests generated by hand.

Here's an Idea for You . . .

Once you've submitted your site to all the major search engines, put a note in your diary for three months from that date. Unless you're noticing that the search engines are visiting regularly, you're going to need to remind them to come again and check out what's new. This isn't spamming; it's common sense. Keep this up for about a year, by which time you'll see that they visit on a regular basis.

 Idea 18

Essential Code?
Meta Robots, etc. . . .

> Talking to robots—your little friends out there in cyberspace—may not be as crazy as it seems. But take care: Not every robot out there wants to be your friend.

Meta Robots

Google pays little attention to your meta keywords, but it's still worth including them if for no other reason than to help you plan out the content of your Web pages. I've come across some Web sites that seem to have an entire constitution and manifesto set up for visiting robots—but if those Web site owners understood how Google operates a little better, it would become apparent to them that a lot of these commands and instructions are pretty redundant. They're better off removed.

When the Googlebot lands on a page of your site, it wants to index that page and then use the links to find out what happens next. So if you notice the command "robots, follow" in your code, get rid of it; you're just slowing the Googlebot down and confusing your message. The Googlebot was going to follow whether you invited it to do so or not.

No Index/No Follow

There might be a reason you don't want Google to concentrate its efforts on certain pages because they are (contentwise) inferior to other pages on your site. If this is the case, it is a good idea to employ "noindex" or "nofollow" and allow the Googlebot to get to the money pages quickly and without hindrance.

Meta Revisit-After

Get rid of it—who are you to tell Google when it should pay you a visit?
The Googlebot will visit when it damn well pleases, and you should be grateful it does. Just make sure that there's something new for Google to index every time it visits, whether it's a new image, some text, or a new page.

Caution

Some robots are written not to scan or index your site; they are unleashed on the Web simply to cause you annoyance by clogging up the server, demanding too many pages too quickly, or generally making a nuisance of themselves. This may well happen to your site, but I wouldn't advise blocking access to robots just because of the threat of malicious activity. The benefits of being open and available to the Googlebot and all the other search engine spiders far outweigh the possibility of a denial-of-service attack.

Here's an Idea for You . . .

Start reading your server log files and actually try to make sense of them. Look out for named robots such as Googlebot and WebCrawler and see what happened when they visited. What pages were accessed? How long did the robot spend on the site? Most important, what pages were not accessed? This will show you whether there are any holes in your navigation and site map and allow you to rationalize the site to be both user- and robot-friendly.

Idea 19

Me in France Number 113
Using Images Correctly

No matter how pretty a picture is, Google can't see it. It can only see the image's file name, and if that says something like "logo.jpg," you've got your work cut out for you.

Toytopia Case Study

If you run an e-commerce store, you need to pay more attention than most to the way images are named. Ensure that every image is named to promote the site and the product to Google rather than just offering a random alphanumeric file name. At Toytopia we had a lot of success with wheeliebugs and carried five different types, each available in two different sizes. Rather than our naming them wheelie1.jpg through to wheelie10.jpg, we used wheeliebug-ride-on-toy-mouse-large.jpg. Part of our success was due to this naming convention.

Not only was this Google-friendly, it made it a lot easier for me to find a specific image within the images folder. When you are carrying hundreds, if not thousands, of products, you'll be pleased you spent a few extra seconds naming each image file correctly. Remember that the text that makes up the image name is adding to the keywords being found on the page. You've mentioned the product a couple of times in your copy, there's a navigational link, and it's reinforced within the file name of the image—Google's beginning to get all dewy-eyed about your site, and that means good positioning on the search results.

Again, taking the example above, logo.jpg is not doing you any favors. Reinforce your brand, your products, and your purpose with something like this: "Toytopia_online_wooden_toys_logo.jpg."

Oh! Big Boy . . .

If you're responsible for uploading images to your site, be aware of the resolution. If you want to print a digital image, high resolution is critical, but for the Web, 72 dots per inch (DPI) is all you require. Any more is wasted information that computer monitors can't process—big images slow down sites and annoy users. Most image-editing software now offers a tool to alter the resolution of an image. Use it.

Here's an Idea for You . . .

If you run a site where a number of members of the staff are adding content, it's time to write a policy or house rules document that outlines the procedure for doing this. Even if you're a one-man band, this is still an important exercise, as it will allow you to check all the existing content and ensure that it's optimized for Google. House style can be as simple as ensuring that paragraphs of text are broken up with the paragraph (<P>) command rather than a break (<BR>), right up to a detailed guide on how to name images, use H tags, and ensure good keyword proximity at the top of the copy rather than the bottom.

Idea 20

Cloaked Content
Being Up-Front with Your Intentions

No matter how good your lipstick and foundation are, Google can see through your thinly veiled disguise—it is far better to try to look good naked.

Seen It All Before . . .

Google is like the aging history teacher you had in high school—coming across all cool and friendly, but if you push the boundaries too much, you'll get an eraser thrown at your head. If you (or your SEO contractor) think you've come up with a great way to trick Google, think again. It's been done, it's been spotted, and anyone else who tries it will be penalized. Google hates cheats, and the penalties can be severe.

Google Means Business

The highest-profile case of Google throwing its toys out of the playpen has to be the German BMW site in early 2006. BMW.de had created a load of keyword-heavy "doorway" pages that

were visible only to the Googlebot; human users would be redirected to a different page. This goes against Google's rules:

If an SEO creates deceptive or misleading content on your behalf, such as doorway pages or "throwaway" domains, your site could be removed entirely from Google's index.

Google's response? BMW.de was effectively removed from the Google index; they no longer existed as far as searchers were concerned. They were given a PageRank of 0, no cached versions of the pages could be found, and there was no mention of BMW.de anywhere within Google. Pretty harsh.

Cloaked Content

Although you may have a legitimate reason for having hidden content on your site, if you can avoid this, do so. The Googlebot is pretty busy with all those billions of Web pages to index and not enough hours in the day. The reality is that Google is not going to ask you questions about your intentions; it's just going to make a decision that is based on the evidence presented. Most Web sites use hidden content for nefarious reasons, and you'll be tarred with the same brush. At best, that page will suffer; at worst, the entire site will be penalized. If you're unsure, don't do it.

Here's an Idea for You . . .

Whether you built the site yourself or employed a developer, take the time to look through the code and pay particular attention to any color commands, especially those relating to text. Your developer might have thought it was doing you a favor by embedding loads of keywords at the bottom of the page in the same color as the background, but Google's just waiting to penalize rule breakers.

 # Idea 21

Content Is King
Building Pages the Right Way Around

Writing good Web copy is hard, but the time you spend perfecting your offering will result in a more successful Web site.

Every Page Should Be . . .

There are exceptions to every rule, but generally speaking there should be at least 250 to 300 words per page. Any less than this and you're going to struggle with effective keyword density and run the risk of "spamming" the page with a long list of keywords that won't make sense to human users.

Support the text with images. This will help break up the page for users and also offer you a chance to drop keywords into the HTML through the naming of the images.

Update your Web pages regularly. Add content whenever and wherever you can. This can involve alterations or additions to the body copy or the inclusion of downloadable files such as PDF or Word documents—but note that Google won't index the copy within these files, so make sure the best stuff is on the Web site itself.

Get your users to add to your content. Offer them a chance to review products or post on

a forum, as this will do wonders for your site. If Google sees new content every time it pays a visit, you'll be rewarded with a higher ranking.

One Phrase per Page

If it's possible on your site, you'll want to create a separate and distinct page for every keyword you are interested in capturing. For example, if you have settled on 15 phrases, you'll need at least 15 pages, and each one should be optimized for that one phrase, using the density rule of about 4 percent. By optimizing each page for one keyword or phrase, you are giving Google a clear indication that each page has a clear and distinct message. That results in individual pages having their own rank on the Google search.

Here's an Idea for You . . .

Don't look at your Web site and think, "I need to rewrite this entire site." Start small and the task will be manageable, so choose your bestselling product or service and begin with that page. Remember keyword density and proximity and the symbiotic relationship between your meta data and your body copy. Fix that page and then pick another one.

 **Idea 22**

Whose Page? My Page!
Owning Page 1

It's all very well being number 1 on Google, but don't sell yourself short—next stop: being number 1, 2, 3, 4, 5, 6, 7, 8, 9, 10.... Here's how.

Stacking the Cards in Your Favor

It's important to buy and/or create keyword-heavy satellite Web sites to capitalize on the words and phrases users actually type into a Google search. Let's say, for argument's sake, you've bought and built seven domains that all have been optimized for their specific target keywords. Now, on top of this, you've been applying many other ideas to your main Web site and three individual Web pages relating to that keyword have been noticed and ranked highly by Google. Great! So what happens next?

You'll have realized by now that your home page is not necessarily the most relevant page for every visitor, and assuming that you've been optimizing, specific pages on your site are being returned by Google. This is the first step toward taking over the world. You see, what you really want to be aiming for is not just to be number 1 on a Google search but to *own* page 1: every reference, all ten natural/organic spaces, and—in an ideal world—all the sponsored listings.

Between the seven satellite sites you've got operating and the three specific Web pages being returned when a user types in a phrase, the net result is that on the surface it appears that the user is being offered a variety of ten separate and independent Web sites. The truth of the matter is that you are behind all of them. It doesn't matter which one they decide to click on; you've got them in your clutches. And your competitors? Well, as you know, if you're not on page 1, you're not in the running.

Resting on Your Laurels

Achieving seven or eight listings on page 1 of Google is not easy; in fact, the more competitive your industry is, the harder it is to do that. Web site optimization tends to become a game involving a few Web sites that all are trying to outdo one another and curry Google's favor. You will see some movement in your rankings (both up and down) as you tweak your site and as your competitors tweak theirs. This is why resting on your laurels is impossible. SEO has to be an addictive habit; you need to return to it again and again or someone is going to knock you off the top spot. Having a number of sites to play with means more work, but you'll have a definite advantage over your competitors.

Here's an Idea for You . . .

If you run an e-commerce store, consider the possibility of launching a new site that sells exactly the same products you sell now, but under a different keyword-heavy domain name and on which the products cost at least 10 to 20 percent more than they do on your existing site. You may be surprised by your increased revenue (for a minimal investment)—and that's two of the ten spots taken up on the Google results page. . . .

 # Idea 23

Face-Off
Posing as Two Different Brands

Alter egos, they say, are a sign of madness. But in the wacky world of e-commerce, you'd be mad not to talk to yourself.

Open Your Mind

One of the most influential people I met during my tenure in the Internet industry (who has asked to remain nameless) was an unassuming chap who approached me after I spoke at a networking event. At the time, my online toy business was doing very well for itself and things were good. I explained my business, its successes, its problems, and generally how everything was going. I was expecting some sort of congratulations or sycophantic praise, but instead he said, "Well, if it works on that one domain, why not launch the same business under a different brand, again and again?" Confused, I asked him to explain and I now have the pleasure of paraphrasing his response.

Dr. Jekyll and Mr. Hyde

If you've proven the business model, your Web site works, and you have a loyal customer base, why settle for one Web site? Yes, there's a cost involved in redesigning sites, paying hosting fees, and setting up new companies—but in the grand scheme of things, considering that all the content, products, reviews, and knowledge already have been collected and documented— how hard would it be to reinvent yourself as your own competitor? I know it sounds a little weird, but think about it: You're always going to have to share page 1 of the Google search results with somebody, so why not make it your alter ego?

Am I Pat or Patricia?

Here's the deal. You have a Web site and a product or service that works. Launch it again, only alter the pricing structure—you can go higher or lower (I would try the for-

mer first). A new brand, a new-look site, a new SEO campaign, and possibly a new AdWords campaign: in effect, two completely different Web sites selling similar products. Lo and behold, you're both competing for the top spot on Google for certain keywords—not a problem—and you've forced a competitor onto page 2. It doesn't really matter whether the user decides to click on and buy from Web site number 1 or Web site number 2; they're both you under different names.

Thinking that I'd successfully mastered this man's advice, I launched another Web site selling exactly the same toys for 10 percent more. It worked really well, and I wrote to thank him for his advice. He replied: "Never mind one extra site; launch 200 sites all selling the same thing—own the product, don't just sell it."

Here's an Idea for You . . .

Dig out the calculator and start working out what it will cost you to launch your site all over again under a different brand. Work out how much you want to increase or decrease your pricing structure and, budget allowing, go for it. If that site works, try another, and another, and another. . . .

Idea 24

How Ya Doin'?
Benchmarking Your SEO Performance

So you think your site's performing pretty well on the search engines? Take a closer look.

www.marketleap.com

Marketleap offers a heap of advice on SEO and search marketing, and it's worth taking the time to read the information. It also offers three powerful tools that are worth trying—and yes, they're free. Let's take a closer look at Link Popularity and Keyword Verification.

Link Popularity

So you've written to all these Web sites and requested an inbound (or backward) link; you might have even received a response that says you're being added. Well, it's time to check. Click on Link Popularity on the Marketleap site and enter your URL, and you'll be able to see how many Web sites link to you and—the best part—who they are.

Now run the same tool but test your competitor's site: Who's linking to that site? It's those Web sites you need to target as they're already proven to be link givers, and I'm guessing they're all pretty relevant to your product and/or service or industry. Thanks for all the hard work, competitor! You also can use www.linkpopularity.com for a similar service.

Keyword Verification

Again, all you need to do is enter your URL and Marketleap does all the hard work. This tool allows you to check quickly whether your site can be found on the major search engines in relation to the keyword or phrase you are querying. If you're not ranked with the first three pages, Marketleap counts this as not being ranked because beyond page 3, your site is as good as invisible to users. What you're looking for is a row of number 1s showing that pages from your site rank on the first page of every major search engine. Most probably you'll see a couple of 1s, a 2, and maybe a "No"—and you can act immediately: Why are you not ranked on Lycos or Netscape? Do you need to submit the site to them? What improvements can be made to your pages to ensure that you're on page 1 across the board?

Run the test for every word or phrase that's important to your site, capture the data as a spreadsheet, and run the test every month. As you continue to implement new ideas, you should start to see a marked improvement.

Here's an Idea for You . . .

Don't look at your link popularity and say, "I need a hundred inbound links, now." That's too overwhelming. Be realistic; try to add inbound links at a rate of one or two a week—that's easier to manage and less depressing.

Idea 25

All Links Are Not Born Equal
PageRank, Relevance, and Are You Trustworthy?

Steer clear of Web sites that offer themselves to you. There's something not right there. Instead, seek out potential partners, target them, woo them, and strike.

Darwin and Natural Selection

PageRank is an important part of Google's ranking algorithm—some would say the most important aspect. The higher your PageRank is, the higher your site will be ranked. The PageRank within your Web site is increased by pages from other sites linking to it, and the higher the PageRank of those pages is, the better it is for the recipient site—you. Thus, in your hunt for inbound links, a handful of links from sites with a PageRanking of 5 or above is going to be of far more intrinsic value than hunting around for hundreds of low-Page Ranked sites. Be selective with your links—ten good ones are better than 100 ho-hum ones.

Yes, but What's the Connection?

With inbound links, obviously a high PageRank is important, but that's not the only contributory factor. There has to be relevance between the content on the Web site that's linking to you and your own site. It's not much good having a Web site with a PageRank of 7 linking to you if you sell T-shirts and the referring site is a hotel directory. There's no connection, there's no relationship, and basically there's no point. . . .

Here's an Idea for You . . .

Believe it or not, there are Web sites out there that actively want links to your site. Type in one of your keywords or phrases and then type "add URL." For example, when I was looking to promote my book *The Bloke's Guide to Pregnancy,* I typed: "pregnancy add URL." I then was presented with numerous Web sites that had some connection to pregnancy and accepted URL submissions. Priceless.

This is a time-consuming exercise. Some sites will want reciprocal links in exchange, some will want to charge you, and some just won't work. Ignore all except the sites that allow you to add your URL with no strings attached—your perseverance will be rewarded. Within 72 hours the number of inbound links will begin to rise, and if any of those linking sites has a high PageRank, you could notice an increase in your own rank the next time the Googlebot pays a visit. You can repeat the exercise by searching for the keywords "add link" and "guestbook" to ensure that you capture all the sites out there offering you a chance to market your site.

Idea 26

No DMOZ, No Champagne Corks
The Importance of the Open Directory Project

Solicit every directory, society, search engine, reference site, and information portal you can—if they're free, all the better. But DMOZ is the undisputed king. . . .

www.dmoz.org

The Open Directory Project is a very unassuming Web site out there in cyberspace that carries a tremendous amount of weight. Its unique selling proposition (USP), ironically in this technical age, implies that it is human-powered and not software-driven. DMOZ doesn't employ spiders to scan the Web. Instead, it waits for you to submit your URL and then assigns an editor to check your listing manually; then, assuming you've added yourself to the correct category, you'll be listed on DMOZ.

What's the Point?

Very few users actually use the directory to conduct searches—why would they when Google does it so much better?—so being listed is not going to affect your traffic levels. DMOZ's data can be downloaded for free, and both small and large Web sites use the data to improve their own sites—and one of those sites is Google. In fact, Google's own directory is nothing other than the DMOZ data.

A successful listing on DMOZ creates two important links to a Web site—one from DMOZ and one from the Google Directory. Both DMOZ and Google have a very high PageRank. Add to this the thousands of links created by all the Web sites that are using the DMOZ directory and it becomes obvious why a listing in DMOZ is so important. It's often the case that a DMOZ listing alone will raise your Page Rank by one or two places!

Patience, Dear Boy

DMOZ's strength is also its weakness. As it is staffed by volunteers, there is a huge queue of Web sites clamoring to get listed; since there are only so many hours in the

day, it can take up to eight weeks for your URL submission to be translated into a listing. Don't send snotty e-mails asking for an update or complaining about the delay; just sit tight and wait. If you've followed the instructions, your turn will come.

Here's an Idea for You . . .

You guessed it: Make it your job this afternoon to get on DMOZ and submit your URL. Read the submission guidelines and choose your category wisely to avoid unnecessary delays.

Idea 27

Google Pretender?
Competition for the Throne

There's loving Google and there's wanting to marry it. I love Google for the instant gratification it can give me today . . . but I certainly wouldn't want to marry it.

www.searchenginewatch.com

The one problem with search engine optimization and particularly with Google is that it is a constantly changing phenomenon. As soon as too many people get wind of a certain facet—take, for example, the current importance of having a DMOZ.org listing—Google eventually will get the idea and alter its algorithm accordingly. For a Web business owner, it becomes a constant game of cat and mouse, forever searching for the latest techniques to beat—no, I mean *utilize*—the system.

The beauty of sites such as www.searchenginewatch.com is that you will get the truth (or at least *a* truth) about what's going on in the world of search engine marketing. Not content with Google's dominance, you can catch up on the latest findings regarding every major

search engine and how it relates to your site. This online community, certainly at the time of this writing, appears to have no political or software manufacturer allegiance—it's simply a meeting place for Webmasters and Web site owners to discuss their experiences and concerns about search engine marketing and promotion. Two weeks of your life would be well spent exploring those posts and researching the archives.

Live Search

I have various personal quibbles with Microsoft, but saying that without mentioning the behemoth and the emerging importance of Live Search would detract from my message: Keep your options open. Live Search has gone through a number of face-lifts recently, but it basically represents a 2.0 version of MSN. Live Search is fast, efficient, and, as far as I am concerned, painfully accurate. Microsoft claims that its technology is unique, and I believe it is; however, I find it difficult to locate a Web site that ranks high on Live Search that doesn't also rank high on Google—which suggests some similarities between the algorithms.

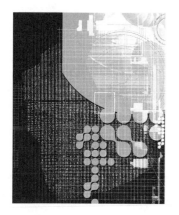 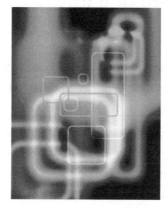 

Here's an Idea for You . . .

It may seem like a waste of time, but it tends to follow that a site that fares well on Google tends to fare well on all the other search engines. Check! Do you really rank the same, if not better, on all the major search engines? Although Google should be your benchmark, don't neglect the competition.

Idea 28

Your Web Site under the Knife
You at the Back, Pay Attention . . .

No one likes criticism, especially if someone else has been paid to do the work, but sometimes Web site errors creep in. Know what those errors are and start erasing them.

Playing to the Stalls

HTML—and Web site design in general—is a pretty organic process. New techniques grow and then become the norm; Web browsers also grow in a bid to display the new code correctly. Conversely, old techniques become, well, old—they no longer are used, and browsers no longer support them. If those techniques have been employed on your Web site, as time goes on, your site will become less and less accessible. So what can you do to stay abreast of what's hot and what's not?

Validate your HTML. You want your Web site to be accessible to the largest cross section of Internet users possible, and this means catering to all tastes and persuasions and not putting all your eggs in one basket. In an annoying way this also means catering to the lowest common denominator: the users who haven't updated their Web browsers or their plug-ins not because they've made a decision not to but because they don't know how. Yet these users could be your biggest customers, and the last thing you want to do is alienate them just because they can't see your site.

W3C.org

This is the self-appointed guardian of HTML. W3C is an influential organization, and a friend of theirs is a friend of Google's. I can't stress this enough: Third-party accreditation and recognition is massively important to Google. If you follow W3C's validation instructions and pass, the validation logo you'll display on your site will be worth its weight in gold in terms of how the Googlebot regards your site from then on.

W3C is pretty picky—for example, I was pulled up on an error regarding one of my sites: The problem was that it wasn't compliant with Internet Explorer version 4 (Microsoft doesn't even support IE 4.X anymore, so why on earth should I?). Take what they say seriously but with a grain of salt—sometimes it's a matter of form over function. If you can fix those errors, do so and enjoy your newfound ally. It's been worth at least a PageRank jump of one place for many a Web site.

Here's an Idea for You . . .

Pay a visit to http://validator.w3.org, type in the URL of your Web site and await the re-sults. If you pass, you'll be provided with a little bit of code that allows you to display the W3C validation logo on your site—I suppose it's the equivalent of ISO 9001 for Web de-sign: a huge accolade and one well worth shouting about. Of course, most of us won't pass on the first try, and W3C kindly provides a comprehensive list of all the errors and, better yet, suggestions about how to fix them. Check out the following validation tools too: http://www.htmlvalidator.com and http://watson.addy.com.

Idea 29

Where Next?
The Site Map and Google

You must do everything in your power to help both waylaid visitors and lost search engines when they find themselves alone and without direction on your Web site.

Do Not Pass Go

Many Webmasters argue that including a site map allows users to bypass their well-thought-out navigation paths and that users therefore aren't subjected to the full, all-powerful magic of the sites. Absolute nonsense. If your visitors cannot find what they want in a very limited amount of time, they are going to leave—and probably not come back. If the Googlebot can't find a way through your Web site, it's not going to hang around too long either, and Google certainly is not going to contact you with a follow-up courtesy call to make sure that everything's fine. You've had your chance.

If you offer a site map, yes, some users may miss out on great offers, witty copy, and stunning images, but they will get to where they want to go. They still may partake in your promo-

tions and appreciate your huge range, but not right now. Be patient. Likewise, if the Googlebot can index your entire site, which it can do easily through a site map, it is going to rank you higher on many more keyword searches. And that's what you want, isn't it? Google can't follow your JavaScript navigation. Employing a site map ensures that there's an obvious link to every page, and the Googlebot will take the easy route if a site map is offered. If your site map is accurate, Google will index every page that is presented.

Help! I Need Somebody

You can never reinforce things too many times on a Web site, and it is therefore a shrewd maneuver to include the site map as part of your

help page, even if it has its own link or button on the home page. Users do not think alike; some will spot the direct reference, and others will assume that you have hidden it within the help pages. Most important, be sure that there is a direct link to the site map from the home page or index page of your site.

Here's an Idea for You . . .

If you don't already have a site map, this issue must be addressed—no matter how small your site is. Even if you have created your site using WYSIWYG (what you see is what you get) software, a map often can be created automatically by the program and added as a page. If developers have created your site, you can ask them to map out the site, as this is information they should have created when they built the site in the first place. Finally, you can get one free at http://www.xml-sitemaps.com in return for advertising their service. If you already have a site map featured on your site, make sure that the locations are clickable and bring the user, and Google, to that page of the site.

Idea 30

Rank and File
How Are Your Keywords Performing?

Pay attention there! It's no good just hoping everything's fine, so find out the truth about how well you please Google, you cheeky minx.

A Leap above the Competition: www.marketleap.com

This Web site probably proved invaluable when you were researching your keywords and phrases earlier on, but the tool we need to focus on now is the keyword verification report. The process is simple: You enter your URL and the keyword or phrase you wish to be measured on, and the report returns whether you rank in the top three pages and on which of those pages you appear—ideally, you want to see page 1 on all six search engines. If your site ranks on page 4 or below, this is deemed as not ranking. Although this is not entirely accurate, the simple truth is that if you're not in the top three pages, it's unlikely that anyone's going to drill down to your listing. Therefore, you don't exist as far as those particular search engines are concerned. Scary, isn't it?

Big Boys' Toys: www.axandra.com

Marketleap is a great tool (not the least because it works and it's free), but you and I are busy people. If you're only interested in monitoring a handful of keywords, it serves its purpose with minimal investment from you. However, most of us are looking to monitor a large number of keywords and phrases, and we would much rather have technology take care of the grunt work. Well, help is at hand. Pop over to www.axandra.com and download its Internet Business Promoter (IBP)/Arelis software for a hard-core version of a keyword performance tool and much more. I can't sing their praises enough; IBP helps you with all-important aspects of on-site Web site promotion. It offers more than 15 professional Web site promotion tools, including tools for keyword generation, a top 10 search engine ranking optimization, search engine submission, directory submission,

ranking checking—and with the Arelis download you'll benefit from highly targeted free traffic to your Web site, new business contacts, a higher link popularity, higher search engine rankings, and more sales. . . . Yes, it's that good.

Here's an Idea for You . . .

The good news is that you can download a limited demo version of IBP to test it out. The demo version allows you to automate your keyword performance, which is what you should do immediately. Once you've tested your performance, you'll know one of two things very quickly—either your site is performing well with regard to your chosen keywords or it's not and you need to bring it up to speed. If you are ranked on page 1 for each of the major search engines, by all means give yourself a pat on the back but bear in mind that the Internet is a constantly changing phenomenon. Someone, somewhere, is gunning for your position. . . .

Idea 31

Number Crunching
Stats, Stats, and More Stats

Number crunching is boring. You might think like this, but whether you like it or not, your salvation and future wealth may lie within a humble spreadsheet. . . .

We should take comfort from the fact that everything can be and is measured on the Web. The trick is to pay attention to all this information and use it. Unlike any other market, the information is there for the taking: statistics about your site, your traffic, your users, where they come from, what they do on the site, and where they go afterward. All this is available if you ask for it and, more important, want to understand it.

www.dataplain.com

Google Analytics is great, but I believe that variety is the spice of life. We have to assume that Google's intentions are morally just, but we also have to bear in mind that it is a profit-hungry business that eats and despises its competition; therefore, we can't be 100 percent trusting of its products. For this reason, if you don't have a stats package as part of your Web site (as well as Analytics), I strongly suggest investing in a third-party package to work alongside Analytics so that you can compare and contrast data. There are many packages on the market, and a search for "Web statistics" will pull up many thousands of offerings. Dataplain is pretty slick, and it's as cheap as fries.

Remember, Not Everyone Uses Google

I'm more conscious than most about rising up the rankings on Google and continually update my sites to stay ahead of the game. My sites rank well on all the search engines, but the truth of the matter is that www.jonsmith.net gets most of its referred visitors from AltaVista and www.justdads.com gets more referred visitors from MSN/Live.com than from Google.

This information is priceless because if my sites were commercial rather than information portals, I would know to commit

my resources to try to get noticed in terms of paid-for listings with Google. Conversely, Toytopia, the online toy shop my wife and I ran, received more than 90 percent of its referred traffic from Google. That's why we spent most of our marketing budget advertising with Yahoo and company—we didn't need to spend much with Google because we were doing so well there organically.

 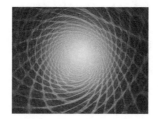 

Here's an Idea for You . . .

Let's say you've decided to spend a modest $3 per day with Google AdWords. Give or take, that's an online marketing budget of $100 per month. Now, if we assume that Google has about 80 percent of the U.S. search market, all the others make up a considerable 20 percent. Match your budget to this trend. Allocate $0.60 per day across the other engines (your stats will tell you who to invest with) and see what happens. Four to eight weeks of activity will ascertain whether it's worth investing more or less—and for the grand sum of about $30.

Idea 32

IP City
Location Management in a Virtual World

Despite the global reach of the Internet, sometimes it's best to call home . . . your home.

Where You Call Home . . .

The sexiest domain name you can own is .com. For whatever reason if it is unavailable you may be left with the dregs. If .net has been taken, give up the search and start again. Investing your money in other domains is a complete waste of time—names like gb.eu.com look clunky, users find them difficult to remember, and there is a suspicion that the business may be questionable. Yes, there are a handful of businesses that have made .biz or .tv a success, but for every one of them, there are at least 500 successful .com sites.

Home and Away

It's very easy to buy domain names from the comfort of your own home. That's the easy part.

The difficult part is ensuring that they are registered and/or hosted in the appropriate country. If you are trying to appeal to a U.S. audience, be sure that your hosting partner's servers are based in the United States. Likewise, if you're after the Irish market, host your Web site in Ireland. Google knows where the servers are and will automatically favor your Web site in that country's search results—and that may not be your target market.

IP and Your User

When users visit your site, unless they buy something, register with the site, or contact you for information, you have no real idea who they are. The only thing they leave behind is an IP address—a numerical code that in crude terms represents the user's computer. This doesn't tell you a lot, but it does reveal the user's location, and that is important. Now, it might not have been your intention, but if the majority of your users are from the United Kingdom or France or Australia, you would do well to relaunch a localized site in those specific countries. If these customers are finding you and using you despite the hidden barriers, imagine the

potential of a site that's optimized for them. Want to know which country your visitors are coming from? Check out http://www.ip2location.com/free.asp.

Here's an Idea for You . . .

Work though your WHOIS details and ascertain exactly where your domain names were registered and, more important, where they are currently hosted. You probably went for the cheapest and easiest option at the time—I did too—but that doesn't mean it was the best option.

Idea 33

Treating Users and Google Differently
E-Commerce and the Session ID Curse . . .

A dynamic Web site is the fastest way to offer good, relevant, and exciting content to your customers, but Google finds a dynamic site hard to index—what should you do?

Who's Your Audience?

You should create your Web site for your user first and for Google second. Sometimes these two separate audiences relate and react positively to the same thing, but your focus should always be on the human user with Google a close second—not the other way around. At the end of the day, although Google may give you the exposure, it's never going to buy anything from you— ever. Talk to your potential client on every occasion while keeping the search engine happy.

Bring the Noise

The problem most e-commerce Web sites have with Google is the sheer vast amount of catalogues or products it carries. We faced the same problem with our toy store—with a modest

150 products. By the time we'd included size options, color preferences, personalization, gift messages, various forms of shipping, and what wrapping the customer would like, we had an enormous database of products, or at least it was enormous as far as the search engines were concerned. On top of that, we wanted to recognize users as they visited the site so that we could capitalize on their next visit—that's why we employed the session ID. That's probably why you've employed it too.

The only problem is that Google doesn't really like the session ID because as far as it's concerned, it means a new page that needs to be indexed even though it has been there before. In fact, the very nature of session IDs is that the same product or page Google has been to before could have infinite session IDs—that's why Google doesn't like them one bit.

Why the Rage?

As far as Google—or any other search engine, for that matter—is concerned, the session ID offers content (which may have been indexed already) at a new location. Every time the Googlebot visits, that content could appear under a different guise and/or session ID, and therefore, rather than wasting resources and maybe double indexing the same information, Google chooses to ignore it. The Googlebot would rather bypass the whole potential mess and turn its back on a page when it spots an "&" in the address.

Here's an Idea for You . . .

Altering the fundamental structure of your Web site is a massive task—but having said that, I still recommend doing it. If it's any consolation, Google acknowledges what a pain in the neck it may prove to be and for the first and only time admits to encouraging what constitutes a "cloaked" page—a page that Google sees as being different from one the general public sees. That means that you can serve a page to the general public with a session ID (so that you can maximize the marketing potential of those customers) while at the same time offering the same page to the Googlebot without the session ID and get away with it. Bizarre, I know.

Idea 34

Web Design #404
"Page Cannot Be Found" Suicide

Click, click, click—ohhh? If I click on a link, I expect it to work. A "page cannot be found" error results in your user abandoning your site, never to return.

NetMechanic

This is a great tool, and if you're happy to check one Web page at a time, it's absolutely free! NetMechanic tests the technical functions of your site, and within a few seconds you will receive some important feedback about how well your site performs. Check out www.net mechanic.com/products/HTML_Toolbox_FreeSample.shtml.

Load Time

How fast is the server serving up the pages? How many servers need to be contacted for the user to download files and images? Are your images optimized for the Web? Although the vast majority of users are employing broadband, they're only so forgiving when waiting for a new site to load. Note that NetMechanic penalizes sites with Web pages over 40K in size, which is a bit draconian. Most important, Google is only going to serve up search results that will allow its customers to get to information quickly.

HTML Check and Repair

This is not as in-depth as the W3C.org facility but is a great starting point in terms of whether the code behind your site is fit for its purpose. If there are errors, NetMechanic will even suggest how to fix them. Google will penalize sites with clunky or error-ridden code. Why on earth would Google want to serve up bad pages to its own customers?

Browser Compatibility

Not everyone uses Internet Explorer (or PCs for that matter), and the number of people choosing to turn their backs on Microsoft products is growing at an astounding rate every month. You and your Web developer need to be aware of how your site looks across all the major browsers because the difference can be enormous. Browsers such as Netscape, Opera, and Mozilla Firefox are all free downloads, and if you're not a convert already, I strongly suggest that you move over to Firefox at your earliest convenience. If you don't have access to a Mac, be sure to have a friend or colleague check out your site by using the Safari browser. If your site looks weird, users aren't going to hang around.

Link Check

Okay, so NetMechanic can't tell if all the links are going to the right page, but what it's looking for are Error #404s—page cannot be found. Broken or dead links are messy, an annoyance for users, and if you serve one of them up, expect to lose that user instantaneously. No one is going to take time out of his or her busy schedule to send you a polite little e-mail highlighting the fault. It's up to you to stay on top of this, and now you have a tool with which to do it.

Here's an Idea for You . . .

You've tested your own site using NetMechanic; now why not use it to spy on your competition? How do they fare in comparison? Is it possible to see a relationship between their current Google positioning and the faults found by NetMechanic? This sort of competitive analysis is priceless yet available for free with a few clicks of the mouse!

Idea 35

How Clean Is Your House?
Nonsmoking, Professional, Clean Code Only

Dig out the marigolds (don't attempt anything without gloves) and get down and dirty, with the code behind your site.

Tidy House, Tidy Mind

Google is a fussy guest; it doesn't want to see flock wallpaper and retro light fittings—it wants to see clean lines, minimal clutter, and impeccably bright surfaces. How does this translate in terms of code? Well, for starters, check out what Google says at http://www.google.com/support/webmasters/, which gives clear and uncompromising instructions on what Google's expecting from your site.

In a nutshell, Google prefers that you present your code in a logical manner—and that logic entails a clear delineation between the showy presentation components of the page and the core content. Google's early visits to your site will be glancing at best, and if your code is presented logically, Google will be inclined to return; if your code meanders, the Googlebot will get bored sifting through the flotsam and jetsam and move on. Less is more.

A Topsy-Turvy Site

This might upset your developers, but it is worth broaching the subject with them in regard to the layout of the code that makes up your site—if at all possible, what you are looking for is almost a reversal of how things normally are done. For example, the classic and, I suppose, the logical way to build a Web page has the same principles as building a house—you start with the foundations, build the walls, put on a roof, and at the last stage deal with putting in some furniture. But bearing in mind the importance Google places on content (read furniture), you might want to give this more importance earlier on in the build. In an ideal world, therefore, after the header information, you want to go straight into content (including keywords, H tags, and Alt tags), and then the architecture—or the showy presentation bit—follows afterward.

Labels, Labels, Labels

Labeling is everything as far as Google is concerned. The Googlebot is looking for flags that accurately represent and showcase the body copy you've used on the page. Tell Google how you've organized the page and what importance you place on certain sections—H, or header, tags work if you prioritize them correctly, along with good use of Alt tags on your images. Rather than splitting text with a simple break (<BR>) command, use a paragraph marker (<P>) and highlight to Google where it should be looking and what the focus should be.

Here's an Idea for You . . .

Pay a visit to the source code behind your site (exactly how you do this will depend on your browser and whether you're using a PC or a Mac). You generally will be presented with a pop-up notepad page showing the code behind that page. Whether or not the content means anything to you, does it look neat and orderly or is it one continuous line of code all jumbled together? If it's the latter, have the developer clean it up.

 # Idea 36

JavaScript Intolerance
Cookies and a Lack of Appetite

You can get all gourmet with Google, offering hand-harvested scallops and fresh basil, but what it wants for its sustenance is a simple slice of toast.

Not a Chocolate Chip in Sight—Call That a Cookie?

An HTML cookie is nothing more than a packet of text sent by the server (along with the page being served up) that immediately is sent back to the server. What it does is allow the site to remember a customer's behavior, patterns, and actions. For instance, if you place a book titled *Web Sites That Work* into your shopping basket, the next time you return, the site recognizes you and that item remains in your basket. Without cookies you'd be regarded as a brand-new customer.

At this level cookies are fine, but what if you've employed cookies to ascertain that someone has signed in or has paid a subscription fee to access certain parts of your Web site? Well, Google can't and won't process cookies and therefore cannot access these "members only" pages. Worse, Google won't give you the benefit of the doubt—it will assume that you are employing cloaking techniques (i.e., one page served up to human users and another served up to Google). As far as Google is concerned, this is inherently wrong, and its reaction is to penalize the site. Avoid cookies where you can.

JavaScript

JavaScript makes navigation sexy, but ironically, it currently cloaks the content from Google's all-seeing burning eye. Basically, Google recognizes how sexy JavaScript can be but also recognizes in its benevolent heart that it might not be accessible to every visitor (those too lazy or ignorant to download JavaScript runtime). Therefore, Google will always penalize JavaScript-heavy sites—unless you have the foresight to incorporate a pure HTML or XML site map, accessible from the home page, that will allow Google to index the entire site regardless of the implementation of JavaScript.

Oh, the Irony

In a strange twist of fate, it has become apparent that users who do not have JavaScript enabled on their Web browsers may find it difficult to access Google's AdWords fully in terms of how the adverts actually are displayed. Why, oh, why is Google so blind to the fact that most Web users are going to want JavaScript-enabled sites? Surely it could incorporate a reader into the Googlebot to acknowledge this and therefore display sites that do employ elements of JavaScript with the same gusto as sites that are constructed out of pure HTML . . .

Here's an Idea for You . . .

So you look at your source code and very quickly realize that all that funky navigation and all those roll-over graphics are wholly dependent on JavaScript. It's going to hurt, it's probably going to cost too, but get rid of them. This is a difficult pill to swallow, but when it comes to the question of to whom you should be tailoring your site, human users can see JavaScript and text-based links, whereas Google can see only text-based links. It doesn't take a genius to work out what has universal appeal. . . .

 Idea 37

The Bigger Picture
Cash-Poor, Time-Poor? Click Here . . .

So you don't have the extra capital to employ an SEO specialist to monitor everything for you? Don't worry; help is at hand.

www.statcounter.com

Yes, this is another stats package that gives you the ability to see what's going on throughout your Web site. Are the keywords and phrases in which you've invested so much time (and possibly money) actually working? Yes, Google Analytics gives you information, but it's truly accurate only for activity on a Google search. Everything else is banded into Yahoo or AltaVista, but if you're investing time and money in these other search engines, you're going to want to know how everything is performing in one glance—and that's what Stat-Counter provides.

Which Search Engines Are Performing for Us?

Google, I've stressed before, is the market leader at the moment and may well be forever more—but also may not be. Don't ignore the old hands and certainly don't ignore the new smaller players as they appear on the market; Google was a small player not so long ago. Keep a close eye on the non-Google stats. Is there a pattern forming, and is traffic increasing, even by just 1 percent a month? They may not be world-beating search engines, but they may be working very well for your site and your business.

Elvis Has Left the Building

What I really like about StatCounter that you don't get with Google Analytics is the exit page analysis. This simply tracks the last page a visitor was reading before he or she decided to abandon your Web site for

new climes. Now, if you run an information-based Web site rather than an e-commerce site, one would hope that the highest-ranking exit page would be your "contact us" page—indicating that the user has gleaned the information required and then found your contact details and either e-mailed you or picked up the phone. Is this the case?

Here's an Idea for You . . .

Something that will work with either StatCounter or Google Analytics is reacting to the visitor location information. It may be that you thought your product would do well in Ireland; you're in the United States, but the products you sell should do really well over there. The truth of the matter is that according to your stats, this is not the case; there seems to be a strong interest in your products in Belgium (of all places!), where customers already are finding you and ordering your product. Imagine how much stronger that offering could be with a bit of page optimization and even a small AdWords budget. Sometimes stats throw your business plan on its head. Although that's a shock to the system—it's always hard to swallow the fact that you might be wrong—let the sales figures be the judge and, your pride aside, react accordingly.

Idea 38

Deep, Deep Down
Understanding the Long Tail

How big is your market? What do people want? Do you even know? When did you last sit down with your customer hat on? What does Google think of that?

The Easy Way and the Long Way

When we all start planning our own businesses, we want to sell what's popular, whether it's a service or a product. The British public likes Teletubbies, so that's what we'll sell. But there's no money in it—out there is a competitor who can either buy the product cheaper or sell it cheaper and still make money. So where does that leave you? High and dry is the simple answer. Think outside of the box: Would that customer also be interested in other educational program merchandise? What about board games, or posters, or rival characters and properties? The long tail is all about taking a theme and working it through to the very end. A customer interested in Harry Potter books also may be interested in a science kit. At first glance it's a tenuous link, but you're not going to compete with Amazon and company selling the book or the DVD, so why not profit from the ancillary products—the magic kit, the magic wand, the magic cape?

Simple Economics

You can spend your life promoting and selling the popular items on your site, but market forces will dictate that you have to sell them at a bigger discount than your competitors—and sell a whole lot more of them—to make a profit because they're so cheap elsewhere. Seek the long tail in terms of what it is you actually should sell. I think your buying skills are intrinsically related to what your attitude should be in terms of how you promote the Web site. Unless you have multi-million-dollar backing, there's no point going for the generic market no matter what your field of expertise is.

Turn to the niche market. It may be small (by definition), but with it comes passion, brand loyalty, and often an obsession that is unequivocal in any other sense. Look at the obsession with sci-fi character figurines—as a hard-core fan, would you wake up one day and buy from a conglomerate such as Toys 'R' Us , or would you buy through a small Web site with a community aspect to it that you've been involved with for the last few months? Even if the same product costs you a few dollars more?

Here's an Idea for You . . .

Return to your keyword analysis. Were there products, phrases, or sentiments that indicated that you could expand or alter your offering? Don't ignore what the facts are even if it goes against the very reasons you decided to set up your company. Profit first, integrity second.

Idea 39

Feeding Hungry Eyes
Forums, Communities, and RSS

A sticky site is one in which users feel happy spending time and feel they have a reason to return again and again.

If you can create a community feeling on your site, you will reap the rewards in terms of numbers of visitors and consumers regardless of what you are selling or promoting on the Web. Google will notice this activity and also will note the many mentions of keywords related to your market on a daily basis. If every time the Googlebot visits, there's tons of relevant, new, and original content, guess what's going to happen to your ranking?

A Home from Home

When it comes to comfort, we would all prefer a soft and luxurious hotel comforter to a starchy, stained motel blanket. This is the feeling you need to replicate for users. Envelop them in your expertise and knowledge, convince the world that your Web site is the definitive provider of information or products, and give them a nice warm feeling—all that makes it nearly impossible for them to leave. When users feel relaxed and at ease, they automatically want to spend more time on your site, and if there is something to buy, hands are going to be reaching into wallets. And never underestimate the power of word of mouth. With the prevalence of chat rooms, discussion boards, forums, and blogs, it does not take long for news to get around. Ideally, users will be so impressed with your site and your service that they will tell all their friends.

We're Not Really in the Right Market for Forums

Cars are easy and popular, but what about my dental Web site or my engineering firm? Well, we're back to a phrase that was popular in the late 1990s—"content is king"—and it really is. If your site has great copy that is updated regularly and is of interest to users, they're going to want to read it. If there's a forum that appears to be well used, they'll be inclined to join in: "I didn't know there were so many people interested in collecting beer coasters." With the invention of RSS feeds, the hard work has been done for you. You post a message or an article, and those who've signed up get a feed—and if there are links on the feed, they come back to visit your site.

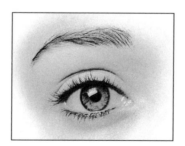

Here's an Idea for You . . .

Look on the Web and find some open source forums that can be downloaded. For starters, you can check out http://www.phpbb.com. Compare the specifications, especially the ability to customize; the appearance (if any) of third-party advertisers; and any issues regarding users having to download a plug-in to take part in the message board. Assuming you have found some suitable software, look to add it on to the site—this could be left hidden from public view until you have configured it, tested the functionality, and filled it with legitimate messages from your huge customer base. Don't think forums are suitable only for B2C (business-to-consumer) Web sites. They can be incredibly effective additions to B2B (business-to-business) sites too by allowing clients to post messages to other clients.

Idea 40

Switching on Targeting Computer . . .
Good and Bad Navigation

The Force may well have worked for Luke Skywalker, but your users are not Jedis. . . . They need to be shown a clear, well-defined path they can follow.

Navigate This, If You Can

Keyword prominence and relevance should be your primary concern in terms of creating effective copy for a Web site, but it all starts with the navigation on the site. You have to be clear and concise in your offering. JavaScript has its place, but Google can't see it. That means that without a site map it can't index your site; the Googlebot will just get stuck on your home page. Graphical representations of buttons look great, but Google can't see the words you added to the graphics, making those links redundant. Simple, honest text links work well for human users and robots. Anything else is actually detrimental to your site and its potential for being ranked.

Irrelevant Navigation

Most Web site design aficionados will sing the praises of keeping the navigation consistent throughout a site to promote familiarity and ease of use, but Google doesn't need to have its hand held so tightly—in fact, it would prefer it if the navigational options altered as it entered different sections or areas of the site. For example, let's say you have a B2C and a B2B offering on your Web site. You will always rank higher on Google if the navigation alters with the section of the site users find themselves in. Your navigation should always be subject-specific and dense in relevant and related keywords. If I'm in the personal banking section of a Web site, there's no need to show me your business banking options—they're irrelevant to me and to Google.

The Three-Click Rule

This dates back to the dawn of the Internet but remains true—your user needs to conclude a visit to your site within three clicks of the mouse. If you're selling products, that third click should be for adding the item to the user's basket. If your site is there primarily to provide information and prospect for new clients, that third click should be to your "contact us" page or to an online inquiry form. If it takes more than three clicks for users to complete their interaction with your site, you must revisit the process.

Here's an Idea for You . . .

Check out any online bookseller and place an order for *Web Sites That Work* or any other book that appeals to you. As you go through the order pipeline (the pages between adding the item to your basket and paying for it), you'll see a very simple graphic at the top of the page that represents the stages involved and where you currently are. Ingenious. A simple device that both reassures users that this process won't take long and serves as a visual hint to where they currently are in the proceedings. Add something similar to your site immediately.

Idea 41

The WORLD Wide Web
Running a Multilingual Web Site Marketing Campaign

Not everyone in the world speaks English. By ignoring other languages, you are in effect blocking potential users from finding and interacting with your business.

Speaking in Tongues

We are very lucky that English often is regarded as the language of both the Net and business, but we have to remind ourselves that not everyone speaks it. Non-English versions of a Web site are not created overnight, nor is the cost of translation cheap. Taking the step to offer a multilingual site or dedicated language versions is something that has to involve all functions of the business and must be budgeted for. The overriding question must be whether a multilingual version of your Web site or the launch of a new country-specific site will add value for both yourself and your customers. If the answer is no, save yourself the project management nightmare and spend the money visiting these far-off climes instead.

Going the Whole Hog

If you decide you need or already have implemented a multilingual site, well done! Multilingual sites are difficult projects to manage and maintain, but the benefits—if they are done correctly—can be immense. Be sure to assign a country manager to each language version of the site or sites. This person will be responsible for the Web site content and updates but, more important, will be your interface with the local Google site. He or she will have to manage keyword selection, optimization, and an AdWords budget if you are planning to pay for placement.

Managing Multilingual Campaigns

Follow the same steps you would for your English-language site. Find out who your competitors are, research your keywords, and begin optimizing the non-English pages. You will need to set up an account with each of the Google territories to monitor your AdWord and Google Analytics; for Spain, for instance, you would start with www.google.es.

Here's an Idea for You . . .

Make a business case for your site to be translated into two additional languages. What would be the benefits to the company, which two languages would be best, and what competition are you facing from Web sites written in those languages and operating in those countries? The plan may show that making your site multilingual is not a viable option. However, it could reveal a huge opportunity (such as there not being a single company selling the same products you sell in the whole of Spain) that could be exploited easily.

# Idea 42

No Rest for the Wicked
Refining, Retuning, Rediscovering . . .

Once most of the hard work has been done, a common mistake is to sit back, hoping the good times just keep happening. They won't unless you stay on top of the game.

Newbie Alert

New players are coming onto the scene every minute. You're probably not the only company selling garden gnomes on the Web, and even if you are today, you won't be tomorrow. Don't rest on your laurels; your great page ranking is good for only that one day—who knows what's going to occur tomorrow or next week?

Why the Fluctuation?

Okay, you've finally begun to reap the rewards—a presence on page 1 of the keywords that are important to you and the increase in traffic and business that you have been after for so long. Then one day you're not there, knocked off your perch and banished to the depths of page 2 or worse. How? Why? Well, don't forget that many of your rivals and any new players in the market who are aware of the importance of SEO will be tweaking their sites too, but most important, the search engines themselves are forever altering their algorithms. Therefore, what was sexy yesterday (think reciprocal links) has been replaced by something else today (think inbound links). Just be aware that the Web and search engines are a constantly changing phenomenon and that it's your responsibility to keep abreast of what's hot and what's not. The Web and the rules that govern it are organic—and it's that very fact that keeps it exciting and incredibly modern but, conversely, incredibly frustrating for Web site owners.

Here's an Idea for You . . .

Every six months (more frequently if you own a large, content-rich site) you should be looking to evaluate and consider your Web site and its performance. Treat the site as you would an employee (regular beatings, denial of holidays, and crackers instead of bakery cookies in the cafeteria). Involve your staff in this process and have them test the site thoroughly. Within a matter of hours you should have a comprehensive "State of the Union" report that can be acted on.

Idea 43

Naming the Child
Web Addresses and the Importance of First Names

Google is very unassuming about what it wants—to be dealing with one Web site on a first-name basis. Anything that deviates from that pattern gets it all flustered.

Registering Births, Deaths, and Marriages

There is a temptation on larger sites to rationalize the pages by creating subdomains to organize the content better—for example, using something like www.business.mydomain.com and www.personal.mydomain.com—but this is counterproductive. Google is much more a fan of first names than of last names and would prefer to see something like www.mydomain.com/business instead, which effectively does the same job for you and your users but keeps a smile on the face of Google. As your business expands and new categories or products make an appearance, you just need to add another page—www.mydomain.com/newpage—and you can have as many as you like.

SKU = Skewed

For ease of management, I'm guessing that all your products and services have been assigned stock-keeping units (SKUs) or product IDs or some form of coding that means that you know what a product or service is but everyone else doesn't, including Google. SKUs are obviously important to any retail business in terms of rationalizing stock, orders, fulfillment, and accounting—but Google and your users have no idea what an F22451 actually is. We'd all much prefer to know that it's a Sony 32-inch HD-ready LCD television, and that has to be represented in the domain name of the page carrying that item.

Yes, but What Do You Mean?

So someone has searched for "Sony 32-inch HD" on Google and is awaiting the results. Less than half a second later the potential customer is presented with a list. If you've named your product with an SKU, the chances of www.mydomain.com/F22451 being returned on page 1 are pretty slim. However, if you've named your page www.mydomain.com/Sony_32inch_HD-Ready_LCD, it's got a far better chance of being shown to that potential user: a potential sale.

Here's an Idea for You . . .

Where it's possible, rename the Web pages that carry the major products and/or services on your site to include the keywords that users actually will employ to find a product. SKUs should be an internal referencing tool, not public information. Keep SKUs private, something management can throw into meetings to appear knowledgeable—"I see sales of 2234 have increased by 20 percent this month"—when the rest of the world would say, "We're selling a lot more bananas this month."

Idea 44

Knowing Google
Dinner Party Secrets You Can Reveal . . .

Google every now and again releases information to assist Web owners in improving their listings. These tidbits are few and far between, so devour them when you can . . . better yet, drop them into conversation with other Web site owners for lots and lots of kudos.

How Do I Know If Google's Been in Town?

Depending on your stat package, you'll see a reference on your stats to the Googlebot or, more likely, see a huge list of IP addresses that don't seem to make a lot of sense. Don't worry! Help is at hand. Here are the IP addresses you should be looking out for—if you see one of these, the Googlebot's paid you a visit:

64.68.80.#
64.68.81.#
64.68.82.#

64.68.84.#
64.68.88.#
216.239.46.#
216.239.38.#
216.239.36.#

Unavailable After

At the time of this writing, the word on the Google grapevine was buzzing around the introduction of a new metatag for Web business owners to employ when they want to flag the fact that they have time-sensitive pages, for example, Christmas offers, month-specific content, or promotional information about an event. The basic idea is that if you have a page on your Web site that has an expiration date, you don't really want that page to be indexed after that date and therefore be re-turned to Google searchers months after the content is no longer relevant. After all, there's no point teasing customers with a potential 20 percent savings on all purchases in December if it's now June and the promotion has ended!

Some Web owners would argue that it's better for an out-of-date page to be indexed and available to potential customers than not, but I don't think that pulling customers in on the promise of a discount that is no longer available or an event that has come and gone is going to win you any friends at all.

Here's an Idea for You . . .

So you've read everything I've written; are you now armed and dangerous? Sort of, but as you've noticed over the last few years, the Web is a constantly changing phenomenon. Just look above to read about the release of a new metatag that was previously unheard of. This will keep happening. The solution? Get involved and sign up to search engine blogs and e-mails to stay ahead of the game. The information is out there—that's the beauty of the Web. Stay on top and stay informed—watch, look, listen: http://www.searchenginejournal.com.

Idea 45

It's My Party
Inviting Links without Seeming Desperate

It's going to require your best poker face—asking for links to your site while giving nothing in return. . . . You could win in the long run.

Phat Spoilers

So I meet with a client who runs a Web site that sells specialist body kits for boy-racer cars—Renault 5s, Subarus, Zafiras, etc.—and things are going well but could be better. We enter into a discussion about inbound links and their importance, and I suggest that the business owner start getting involved in forums relating to his industry. "But I'm already a member of loads of them," he replies.

And he isn't joking. Over the last three or so years he's done somewhere in the region of 5,000 posts across a whole load of forums and chat rooms. Now, the beauty of forums is that more often than not they allow the user to create a profile, and one of the fields is URL. Most people leave this blank or add a link to their Facebook/MySpace page—such a waste. Add your company Web site address. In the case of the company mentioned above, he sold kit parts for cars, and here he was chatting on performance-car-related sites. He quickly added the URL of the business to his profile, and, being dynamic, the forums updated every post this guy had ever placed on their sites with a link to his own Web site. With over 5,000 inbound relevant links to his credit, his site became an authority site overnight with a PageRank of 7. From page 8 to page 1 in 24 hours. It brings a tear to my eye.

Beware: Cash for Honors

It has damaged the major political parties, in the UK and it could affect you too—there is an increasing trend for Web sites with a high PageRank to prostitute themselves to the highest bidder. Never mind selling a $10 DVD when you can sell your Google reputation for dollars and dollars and dollars. Google is wise to this tactic, and though I don't fully understand how it

could know that you and I exchanged a brown envelope in a service station café on the interstate, it does. Buying inbound links is a short-term fix, and you'll be found out, which inevitably will

lead to all the punitive measures Google has at its disposal. Get to your goal through your own strengths and Google will reward you.

Here's an Idea for You . . .

If it hasn't dawned on you already, search the Web for a forum that's related to your industry. There's something out there for every taste and persuasion, and if there isn't, that's your cue to add a forum or blog to your own site. I'm serious. Even if you run a Web site that focuses on welding, there's a potential market out there that would be eager to get involved; they're just waiting for a suitable venue. Become the authority site.

Idea 46

Yahoo! and Industry-Specific Directories
Entering the World of Other Search Engines

Although Google is the daddy at the moment, this could change very rapidly. Make sure you're listed on every search engine and directory.

Entertaining the Masses

The other search engines are not to be sneezed at—it's all very well being number 1 on Google, but truth be told, although 80 percent of the search market is Google-led, that still leaves a massive one in five Internet searchers who choose not to use Google for whatever reason. Are you just as high on Live.com, Yahoo!, or AskJeeves? If not, work on figuring out why not. Theoretically, if you rank highly on Google, you also rank highly on the others—but that isn't always the case. In the past, to be honest, I had sites that have ranked highly everywhere *but* Google.

Business Directories

They're out there and they are used—they just don't advertise themselves very well. Every city or county government will have a register or list of companies and businesses in the area, and most offer a chance for you to add yourself or at least alter the information held on your business. I still receive queries via Bedford City Council's site from people interested in Toytopia Ltd.; the business was sold four years ago and ceased trading soon afterward, yet they still come. These sites do work, so be sure you and your business are listed.

Twice-Weekly Bin Collections . . . and Your Web Site

So we all hate our local governments—unruly youths allowed to roam the streets knocking off wing mirrors and throwing empty bottles of beer into your yard . . . they're awful! But that said, the departments that look after social issues are completely different from the ones that are interested in promoting local businesses, local interests, and local innovation.

Use and talk to your local government about what it is you are doing as they're always eager to sing the praises of businesses within their region. At worst they'll add you to their directory, which is another inbound link; at best, they will shower you with business advice and assistance (possibly financial) and will try to sing your praises (to make themselves look better) to the local press—which can only mean good exposure.

Here's an Idea for You . . .

Run a report through www.marketleap.com and take a look at which search engines have and haven't picked you up. I can't stress this enough: Although Google is the daddy at the moment, this could change very rapidly (probably through copyright holders suing for billions of dollars now that Google owns YouTube). Pay as much attention to your listing on AltaVista, AskJeeves, and so on, and you'll be ready for whatever revolution is about to happen. Make sure you're listed on every search engine and directory.

Idea 47

Negative Press
Being Dissed on the Web

No matter how well you promote your business and your site, someone, somewhere may have it in for you: a disgruntled customer, an ex-employee, an obnoxious member of the public. . . .

Disgruntled customers, whether they've explained their problem to you or not, may decide to use the Web to vent; sometimes they'll write negative comments about a company in their blogs. Some of your competitors might like to damage your reputation by creating fake comments about your site.

No matter how good your company is, some people will write something negative about your site even if you tried your best to help them. What can you do if Web pages with negative comments appear on the first result page for your company name?

Ask and Thou Shalt Receive . . .

That is not as unlikely as it might appear. All Webmasters are conscious of rankings and SEO and are striving to be the highest in their own field. If you send the Webmaster of the Web page in question a polite e-mail and ask for the removal of the negative comments, he or she may agree—especially if this is a portal or forum site in which he or she has no control over the quality or accuracy of the comments submitted. Be friendly, polite, and self-effacing and don't ever threaten the other person. Many Webmasters will cooperate if you explain the issue.

Give Web Pages with Positive Comments about You a Boost

Find Web sites that contain positive comments about your site, whether they are links, comments, or testimonials. Link to those pages from your own site to increase the link popularity of those particular pages. The Web pages with the positive comments may get more inbound links

and higher rankings, thus forcing them to leapfrog over the site with the negative comments. Granted, this is counterproductive to establishing your site as the number 1 site, but if you're a long way off, better the devil you know. . . .

Wikipedia

Web sites such as www.AboutUs.org allow you to create an article about your own company. If your company is regarded as important enough, you may even find that a page is created as an entry in Wikipedia. These "Wiki" pages will be returned when someone searches for your company name. Having a reference on Wikipedia is tantamount to being featured as a guest voice on *The Simpsons*—it means you've made it culturally. You're now a talking point and soon will enjoy your own listing in the *Oxford English Dictionary*. None of this is guaranteed, of course, but you never know. . . .

Here's an Idea for You . . .

Okay, so it's frowned upon, but who is going to create a page about you on Wikipedia other than yourself? Fine, that's settled. It's pretty clear that you're the one who's going to have to do it. Learn the ropes, read the FAQs, and start creating. Be sure to register with a name and an e-mail address that is not related to your company and be sure to back up every fact and statement with a legitimate Web link, source, or external reference that can be verified.

Idea 48

What? Explain!
SEO in a Nutshell

This is all very well, but if you could summarize what it is I have to do to make my site rock. . . .

The German company Sistrix took it upon itself to analyze Web page elements of the top-ranked pages in Google to find out which specific elements lead to high Google rankings. They analyzed 10,000 random keywords, and for every keyword they analyzed the top 100 Google search results.*

Which Web Page Elements Lead to High Google Rankings?
Sistrix analyzed the influence of the following elements: Web page title, Web page body, headline tags, bold and strong tags, image file names, images Alt text, domain name, path, parameters, file size, inbound links, and PageRank.

Keywords in the title tag seem to be important for high rankings on Google. It is also important that the targeted keywords be mentioned in the body tag, although the title tag seems to be more important.

*Source: www.Axandra.com.

Keywords in H2 to H6 headline tags seem to have an influence on the rankings, whereas keywords in H1 headline tags don't seem to have an effect.

Using keywords in bold or strong tags seems to have a slight effect on the top rankings. Web pages that used the keywords in image file names often had higher rankings. The same seems to be true for keywords in image Alt attributes.

Web sites that use the targeted keyword in the domain name often had high rankings. It might be that these sites get many inbound links with the domain name as the link text.

Keywords in the file path did not seem to have a positive effect on the Google rankings of the analyzed Web sites. Web pages that use very few parameters in the URL (?id=123, etc.) or no parameters at all tend to get higher rankings than do URLs that contain many parameters.

The file size doesn't seem to influence the ranking of a Web page on Google, although smaller sites tend to have slightly higher rankings.

It's no surprise that the number of inbound links and the PageRank have a large influence on page rankings on Google. The top result on Google usually has about four times as many links as does result number 11.

Here's an Idea for You . . .

> Look at or have your developer look at the use of or lack of use of header keywords in the code behind the site. If you have a number of H1 tags, look to split them up, in order of importance, into H1 to H6 tags. If there are no header tags at all, create some immediately but don't give all of them the H1 status; sometimes less is more.

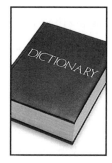

Idea 49

Google AdWords
Pay to Be First

I've followed the advice, and now I'm visible on page 1; I might even be the number 1 site for certain keywords. What can I do next?

Why AdWords?

Google, you must remember, is a business. It does not provide a powerful search tool and employ thousands of staff members around the world for fun. There are shareholders to appease, and that means Google needs to make money. Unlike other search engines, Google had a different approach from the start; its home page has always been dedicated to Google tools, not big-spending advertisers. This clean, uncluttered approach immediately made it attractive to users intent on searching. So where does it make money?

What Google has done with AdWords is essentially create an online auction of every word and phrase in every language—pretty incredible. No one's obliged to take part, but human nature is competitive (and lazy); therefore, when we see a competitor sitting proudly at the very top or on the right side of a search results page, we want to be there too. The more popular a keyword is, the more the price goes up—this is how Google makes its money: Hundreds of thousands, if not millions, of businesses around the world, big and small, are paying their pennies and dollars for a little cameo in the top tier.

www.google.com/adwords

Setting up is really simple, but do take the time to read the help and FAQs provided on the site. Google knows how its system works and has taken the time to explain it all; it just requires you to sit down, uninterrupted, to read through the data and see how it applies to your Web site and your industry. AdWords does work, but depending on your industry, the current price for some keywords (such as "Business Consultant" and "Microsoft Software Training") can be so high that it's prohibitive.

AdWords works by charging you a fee that you've decided on every time someone clicks on your ad. The more you are willing to pay, the higher up the sponsored links you will be placed, and the bigger your daily budget is, the more users will be shown your advert and the more who will (one hopes) click through. When your budget has been spent, your ad is taken off until the next day. This allows businesses to keep tight control of their online marketing spend and also allows you to see very quickly whether the campaign is working and judge your return on investment.

Here's an Idea for You . . .

Set yourself a really low budget, say, $1 per day, and your ad will be shown until that budget has been spent. Again, it can't do you any harm to be working with Google.

 # Idea 50

I'll Make You Number 1!
The Dangers of SEO/AdWord "Specialists"

> Where there's an opportunity, there's an opportunist. . . . The tools and techniques being offered by SEO "specialists" are those contained here and are probably not even this exhaustive. . . .

An Expensive Business

Web developers, designers, and engineers have enjoyed hallowed ground immunity for many years. The impenetrable black art of Web site creation has proved to be a fortress to which most of us mere mortals simply do not hold the key. We've been reliant on their views in terms of the look, feel, and design of our Web sites for so long that we've gotten used to it—and they've gotten used to it too.

I'm not for a moment suggesting that Web developers are without value; far from it. They offer a service for which you pay, and more often than not, you'll receive a decent product in return. But they are looking to expand their portfolio of incomes, and what better way than to hit existing customers with extra products and services—namely, SEO: "We've built your site; now let us take it to the next level. . . ."

Outsourced SEO can cost anywhere between $100 and $1,000 a month. The question is, Do your returns justify this expenditure? How much of it can you now do in-house and, more important, how much do you want to do in-house?

Taking the Hit

Now that you're armed with the knowledge, the techniques, and the lingo, it may prove cost-effective to employ a third party on a monthly basis to look after your SEO while you get on with whatever it is you do best, depending on your turnover and staffing levels. Only you will know the answer to this. For some businesses it does make financial sense to employ a third party. Now you know the questions to ask and the language to use and have a mental checklist of all the things you should, quite rightly, expect to be delivered. The balance has altered. Although you may opt to remain a customer, you are now a very informed customer.

Here's an Idea for You . . .

This may be morally wrong, but we're talking about business, not charity. Take a look on the Web or get recommendations through contacts at the firms offering SEO improvements. What are they offering? What assurances are you receiving? What will they do as a sweetener to get you involved? Without fail insist on at least a month of demonstrable improvement to your listings before parting with cash and sit on them to make sure they still are looking after your site once that money has changed hands.

Idea 51

Is This Working?
User Testing to Monitor Your Search Results

Testing and retesting are fundamentally important to the success of your search engine marketing. Companies that choose not to test may as well sit there and smoke $20 bills.

The Truth Hurts

User testing does take time. It can cost, but nowhere near as much as the cost of failure. Your testers' comments at best will make you disappointed and at worst will mean rethinking your entire search engine marketing strategy. However, if testing is done professionally and continually, you will reap many rewards. User testing must go outside the walls of those with a vested interest in the success of the site. If you all have the same paymaster, there is bound to be some bias, and that is not going to give you the honest and reliable feedback you need from Joe Public or from the girl on the street with nothing better to do on a Tuesday afternoon. . . .

What Is to Be Done?

Testing can be done on a shoestring, and anyone who knows what the Internet is will do as a tester. Prepare a brief for your testers; introduce them to the company and the Web site and explain what you want from them. Set specific search tasks—for example, if you run a Web site specializing in villa vacations, you'll want one tester to be searching for destinations ("villa Cancun," "villa Spain," etc.) and another tester to be searching for the industry ("villa," "vacation," "self-catering," etc.). Compile the results—your position on the page, the position of competitors, your AdWord campaign listing position if applicable, and so on.

By all means have a number of testers working on the same search terms, but treat them like defendants in a police interview: Don't let them meet and don't let them compare notes. Only when the testing is complete should you see what, if any, correlations can be drawn.

If possible, have testers around the world, as the results can vary drastically with the IP address of the Web browser making the search. If you do trade (or wish to trade) globally, this is essential.

Here's an Idea for You . . .

If you have a set of testers available when you're developing a new keyword-specific destination page, get them to give you their comments about whether the page "answers the question." If, for example, you are selling a new skin cream high in aloe vera, ask your testers if the page does what it should—explain the importance of aloe vera, show why your cream is better than the others on the market, and explain where and how users can order. This third-party viewpoint can be invaluable. Pay attention to any other comments testers might have about color, layout, ease of use, and the like. They might all focus on what seems like a banal point— "I don't really like that shade of green," "Looks a bit like such and such.com," and so on—but this is what user testing is all about. By fixing the little problems, you will make your site great.

Idea 52

I Am/Am Not King of the Hill
A Word of Warning

Take a look at me now! King of the hill, number 1 on a global search for any key-word you care to think of—I own the Web. . . .

Who's Your Daddy?

So, with your newfound SEO obsession, it's all come together and you're sitting pretty in the number 1 spot. Well, you can be assured that someone else covets your space and is going to be looking for ways to beat you down. Do not lose sight of your goals, ever. The Web is constantly changing. New sites pop up every day and old sites drop off without so much as a good-bye, but the number 1 spot is always the most coveted. Your competitors covet it with as much venom as you once did, if not more—all those weeks or months ago.

Equally, search engine optimization takes time. This is not a quick-fix overnight tweak that means that come tomorrow morning, your Web site will be more popular than eBay or Amazon or YouTube. For a start, it's going to take a few weeks for Google to send the Googlebot to your site (whether you request it or not)—there are millions of sites out there craving the attention of Google and company, and the process takes time. Don't loose heart. If you play by the rules, increase the number of inbound links from relevant sites, keep your site updated and relevant, and constantly monitor, measure, and react, your site will get a high rank. In business, patience is something we all lack.

Hang On! Yesterday I Was on Page 1, Today I'm on Page 13!

Google and, to a lesser extent, all the other search engines also are tweaking their service constantly. It is very clear that when Google alters the algorithm once too many times people figure out what makes certain sites rank high (which has led inevitably to abuse). Five years ago it was all the rage to have as many reciprocal links as you could; now Google is interested only in inbound or backward links. In six months the algorithm will alter again, and all we can do is adapt and try to keep up. The important thing is that all the ideas here will help you rank high on Google and all the other search engines and continue to do so in the years to come. It is your responsibility as a Web site owner to keep up to date with what's hot and what's not.

Here's an Idea for You . . .

When you've been improving how you rank with Google for about a year, it's time to take stock and, more important, look toward the new year and the business challenges it will bring. However your performance has been, type in your most treasured keyword, find the first reference to your site, and print the page—this is your baseline. For the next 12 months you need to maintain that position or improve on it. Print the page, stick it up on the wall, and spend each and every day employing these techniques and rising up the rankings.

Index